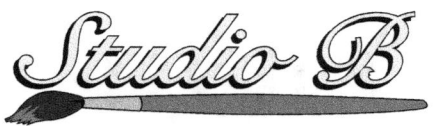

Edited by Jane E. Stahl and Published by Susan Biebuyck
Volume Eight
Printed in 2021

———————————

© 2021 Stahl/Biebuyck All rights reserved.
R. R. Bowker - US ISBN Agency
ISBN: 978-1-7345833-1-1

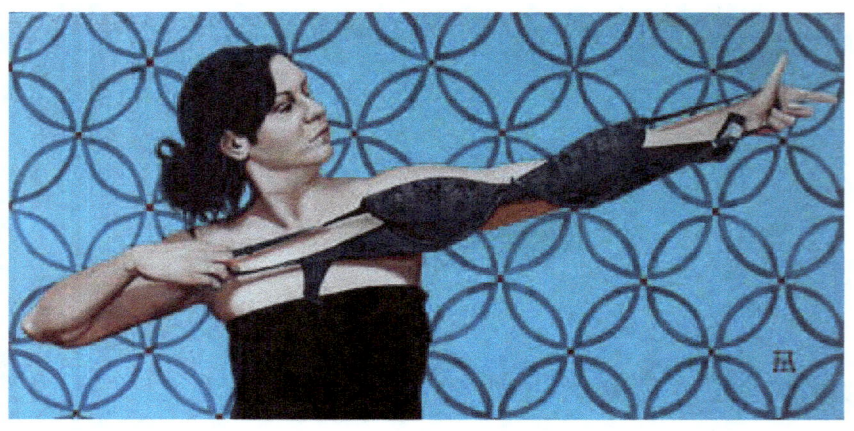

"Best Part of the Day" oil   *Angela Izzo*

Preface

~Jane E. Stahl

What better way to survive the angst and turmoil of daily life—and the historic challenges we have faced personally, nationally, and globally in recent years—than to focus on the things we love? Our "favorite things" save us in many ways on many days; they provide meaning and motivation. To enjoy them, we are required to stick around—dissolving into a dew just won't do!

Today while much remains the same to keep us somewhat sane—the world is still spinning; the sun comes up each day and goes down each night, and there are familiar distractions like dishes and laundry to do and meals and beds to make—the challenges we've been facing in recent years seem overwhelming. The pandemic is still killing us, the lockdown is still keeping us distanced from each other; we're still wearing masks; hoarding toilet paper, and avoiding most people, most of the time.

The trauma we've undergone and the post-trauma stress we're feeling from a daily onslaught of bad news from many corners—sickness and death, partisan division, broken relationships, threats to our democratic way of life, fires, floods, fear and hatred—so much hatred—has changed our lives—inside and out.

And while we're hoping someday soon to be "free" to roam and hug our friends and family and vow never to speak about all the absurdity we witnessed in 2020 (and early 2021), our change is a disturbing realization that things—and we—aren't what we thought…or hoped…we were—as individuals, as family members or friends, or as a country.

"I thought we were better than this!" is a refrain I've heard often and said myself as we've watched violence play out on our streets, in our Capitol, and sadly, in some cases, within our own families--violence in word and deed born out of a rejection of others because they are different from us or represent an unwelcome transformation of some kind.

The sadness is real and reminds me of the sadness of 9/11/2001* following the fall of the Towers. Then, we were assaulted by events largely out of our control by people from the other side of the world. We lost our innocence—a confidence that this kind of assault would never happen on America's shores. We learned clearly that the world was not as good as perhaps we thought it was; we were not as safe as we'd assumed. We learned that the motivation to destroy and hurt innocent people was very real and very much alive; we learned that other people couldn't be trusted, and we should fear them.

But the saddest part today is that today the assault comes from within our own country, from our fellow Americans, and to some degree from our own friends and family members. We're aware that evil competes easily with hope and enthusiasm. We've lost yet another level of innocence, and we are grieving.

Still, just as in 2001, this sad time affords us an uncommon opportunity to refocus, to look at life differently, to reorient ourselves to a "new normal," and an uncommon opportunity to change ourselves, our priorities, our activities, our relationships. And it forces us to savor those beauties in our lives that bring us joy forever: our favorite things.

And so, we bring you images of beauty, reflections of moments in our lives of people, places, things, and ideas of courage and hope and dignity and love that help all of us to conquer the nagging fear and isolation and seeming futility of which life is made.

Years from now as we all remember this time; we'll be able to see more clearly who we were before and after these traumatic times. We'll understand a little better why joy and laughter came a little harder; trauma and grief stood in our way.

But joy will come again. Our favorite things offer beauty to us forever. And perhaps my favorite things are also some of yours. May you be inspired by the sharing our area writers and artists offer in this volume, "My Favorite Things: Beauties Are Joys Forever."

****

Flowers—all kinds and colors—ferns, tall grasses and trees, succulents, the myriad textures of leaves and stems and lichens and bark. Love 'em all.

And dogs—I love all kinds of those as well.

I love the mossy carpet that covers the ground under the shade of my maple tree.

I love the single leaves, tiny tri-colored ones, that begin to fall at summer's end.

In autumn I love that same mossy lawn that turns rose-colored with fallen maple leaves.

And I love the palm-sized leathery oak leaves that hang on through November.

I love the smell of fresh-mowed grass and the first cup of coffee each morning.

I love cozying up with the morning newspaper before anyone else knows dawn has arrived.

I love a hot shower, loose-fitting pajamas, and, yes, changing into comfy clothes at the end of a workday leaving binding apparel behind.

I love weeding after a rain. And the solitude I can count on, close to the earth, when my people stay clear of me, to avoid an invitation to join in my "fun."

As a former teacher, I still love "snow days."

I love a leisurely ride in the country, long road trips that take me from Pennsylvania's dirty snow packs to Florida's Royal Palms.

And I love coming home from a vacation to my own bed.

I love streams and lakes and oceans and my pool—the look and sound of rippling streams, cool water in summer's heat, the reflections of sunlight that dance on nearby walls and ceilings.

I love being barefoot, on beaches, in cool grass, and on warm sidewalks in early May.

I love wild summer storms but also the sound of my sump pump keeping water out of my basement.

I love the silence of a snowy winter night, the glisten of new-fallen snow, the peace of solitary moments while shoveling.

I love the lengthening days, the morning sunbursts, and the slant of sun in February, signaling the approach of spring.

And daffodils. Bright. Yellow. Bursts of sunshine, promises of spring.

"I thank you god for most this amazing/ day.... (now the ears of my ears awake and/ now the eyes of my eyes are opened)"

~ ee cummings

On September 11, 2001, 19 militants associated with the Islamic extremist group al Qaeda hijacked four airplanes and carried out suicide attacks against targets in the United States. Two of the planes were flown into the twin towers of the World Trade Center in New York City, a third plane hit the Pentagon just outside Washington, D.C., and the fourth plane crashed in a field in Shanksville, Pennsylvania. Almost 3,000 people were killed during the 9/11 terrorist attacks, which triggered major U.S. initiatives to combat terrorism and defined the presidency of George W. Bush.

CURATOR'S PREFACE

~Susan Biebuyck

Annus horribilis pronounced an·nus hor·ri·bi·lis
The expression was brought to modern prominence by Queen Elizabeth II. In a speech at Guildhall on 24 November 1992, marking her Ruby Jubilee on the throne, she said:
"1992 is not a year on which I shall look back with undiluted pleasure. In the words of one of my more sympathetic correspondents, it has turned out to be an annus horribilis."

I was on my bike in 1977 when a friend told me that Elvis died. My parents were so upset. I didn't get it.

John Lennon was shot and killed December 8, 1980. I was in the 9th grade and the entire school was in tears. I was too but I was in love with Paul.

Annus horribilis was the term I learned the year that Princess Diana was killed in a car crash with her boyfriend Dodi Fayed. It's a stark memory for me. I'd followed her wedding in my senior year of high school. She was beautiful and had everything. I was sad for her and her sons. I watched the funeral in tears while Elton John played "Candle in the Wind" and millions of people lined the streets to watch her funeral.

And, frankly, I'm really feeling this year of Corona Pandemic. From March 2020, through now April 2021, at the start of design of this book, I have lost several friends, lost a couple of dear artists: Bonnie Wren and Ineke van Werkhoven. I had to put my dear precious cat Lucy to sleep at a veterinarian who was less than gentle just so I could be with her when she passed. And finally I lost my Mom. What a crushing blow this 12 months has been.

And then there's Jane, searching for the pretty things. Bringing me and hopefully all of us back to a place of Joy. In this book, I hope art is a place for you to rest your eyes, enjoy the colors and forms that reflect the writing. Often it is tragic loss and destruction that brings forth the most emotional artistic response. Sometimes it takes a good cry to feel a little better. Remember, we at Studio B are here to support art, artists, writers, musicians and all creative people.

Air hugs, sigh.

"I Don't Like Mondays"
Song by The Boomtown Rats

The silicon chip inside her head
Gets switched to overload
And nobody's gonna go to school today
She's gonna make them stay at home
And daddy doesn't understand it
He always said she was good as gold
And he can see no reasons
'Cause there are no reasons
What reason do you need to be shown?
I don't like Mondays
(Tell me why)
I don't like Mondays
(Tell me why)
I don't like Mondays
I wanna shoot the whole day down
The Telex machine is kept so clean
And it types to a waiting world
Her mother feels so shocked, father's world is rocked
And their thoughts turn to their own little girl
Sweet sixteen, ain't that peachy keen
Now it ain't so neat to admit defeat
They can see no reasons
'Cause there are no reasons
What reasons do you need, oh oh oh oh?
I don't like Mondays
(Tell me why)
I don't like Mondays
(Tell me why)
I don't like Mondays
I wanna shoot the whole day down
Down, down, shoot it all down

And all the playing's stopped in the playground now
She wants to play with the toys a while
And school's out early and soon we be learning
And the lesson today is how to die
And then the bullhorn crackles and the captain tackles
With the problems and the hows and whys
And he can see no reasons
'Cause there are no reasons
What reason do you need to die, die, oh oh oh?
The silicon chip inside her head
Gets switched to overload
And nobody's gonna go to school today
She's gonna make them stay at home
And daddy doesn't understand it
He always said she was good as gold
And he can see no reasons
'Cause there are no reasons
What reason do you need to be shown?
I don't like Mondays
(Tell me why)
I don't like Mondays
(Tell me why)
I don't like
I don't like
(Tell me why)
I don't like Mondays
(Tell me why)
I don't like
I don't like
(Tell me why)
I don't like Mondays
(Tell me why)
I don't like Mondays
I wanna shoot the whole day down

"I Don't Like Mondays" is a song by Irish new wave group The Boomtown Rats about the Cleveland Elementary School shooting in 1979 near San Diego. It was released as the lead single from their third album, <u>The Fine Art of Surfacing</u>. The song was a number one single in the UK Singles Chart for four weeks during the summer of 1979, and ranks as the sixth biggest hit of the UK in 1979. Written by Bob Geldof and Johnnie Fingers, the piano ballad was the band's second single to reach number one on the UK chart.

Bob Geldof & Johnnie Fingers
"I Don't Like Mondays" lyrics © Universal Music Publishing Ltd.

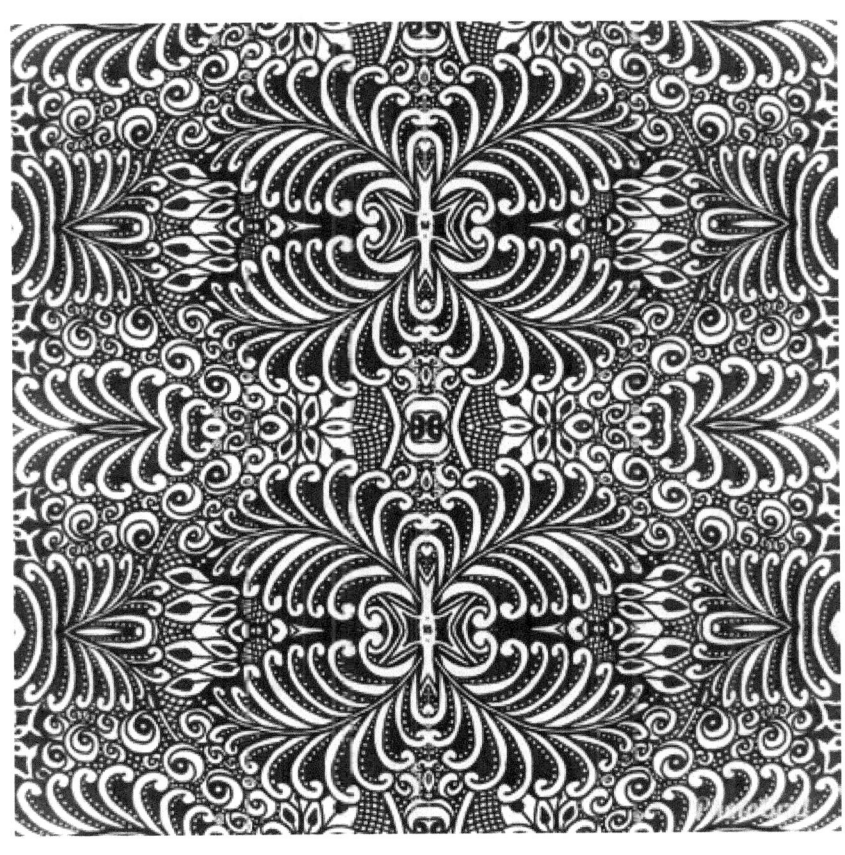

"Curly Doodle" ink　　　　　　　　　　　　**Beth Glick**

Table of Contents

PREFACE
Jane E. Stahl 5

CURATOR'S PREFACE
Susan Biebuyck 9

NANCY LANG BOYER
Dedication 21

THE TRUE MEANING OF "FARM"
Claudia Bahorik 23

WHAT MAKES ME HAPPY
J. Wesley Bahorik, Ph.D. 27

LEADING GUIDED MEDITATIONS
Rev. Michael Barnett, M, Div., M.Ed. 31

MAKING VIBRATIONAL HEALING ART
Rev. Michael Barnett, M, Div., M.Ed. 33

THE LOUD BOUQUET
Marilyn Basehoar 35

INSIDE THE KALEIDOSCOPE
Virginia Beards 37

THE LADY BIRDBRAIN SCULPTURE
Virginia Beards 39

THE MYTH OF APOSTROPHES
Craig Bennett 41

WE DANCE
Krysta Bernhardt 45

FORGOTTEN
Cathryn Clinton 49

DAYCLUB
Tony Cocuzza 51

SAVED
Tony Cocuzza 53

ZERNS FARMER'S MARKET
Carole Croll 55

BLESSED BEE BALM
Kimberlee Dawn 57

THE MOSS
Stacey Dexter 59

OUR TRYING TIME
Jon Egger 63

MY FAVORITE THINGS
Andrew Fritz 65

MY MOTHER'S PICTURE
Jennifer Gittings-Dalton 67

TO SWIM WITH LILIES
Heather Goodman 71

THE TRANSFORMATION OF AN OLD FRIEND
Walt Hug *(aka The Tree-Hugger)* 75

FINDING HAPPINESS IN A DIFFERENT WORLD
L.T. James 77

ALTAR
Kathryn Keegan 79

SIMPLE MARVELS
Kathryn Kirk 81

A*PART
Kathryn Kirk 82

GRAND
Kathryn Kirk 83

THE GREEN MAN
Marilyn Klimcho 85

THINGS THAT SHINE
Virginia McNamara 87

DNA
Lesley Huss Misko 91

BLOOMS STAND TALL
Lisa Mitchell 95

HAZEL
Clemson Page 97

PERPETUATE
Philip Repko 103

A BRANCH OF ME
Philip Repko 107

REUNION
Philip Repko 111

MY JOURNAL
Theresa Rodriguez 115

STEINWAY PANTOUM
Theresa Rodriguez 117

ATTITUDE ADJUSTMENT
Christine Ross 119

IF ONE WOULD JUST TAKE THE TIME
Ashley Rupert 123

MORE THAN A MERE REFLECTION
Ashley Rupert 125

FIRST SNOW
Michael Schiffman 127

WHAT IS A PANDEMIC?
Michael Schiffman 129

BARE FEET
Sandra Seaman 131

LIGHT AT THE END OF THE TUNNEL
Sandra Seaman 133

NO GIFTS PLEASE!
Jane Stahl 135

A GREETING
Jane Stahl 141

BOTTOM TO THE TOP
JD Stahl 143

INSPIRATION
JD Stahl 147

HUMHA: THE MONSTER
Taku, known as **VaChikepe** 149

SAN MATEO 1943
Ted Thomas 153

SUNDAY MORNING
Ted Thomas 155

JIGSAW PUZZLES ARE MY ADDICTION
Nelvin Vos 157

GIRLFRIENDS
Aressa Williams 163

MY FAVORITE THINGS
Sandra Williams 167

AFTER
John Yamrus 171

I SAT IN THE SUN ROOM
John Yamrus 173

Art & Artists' Index

"Best Part of the Day"	**Angela Izzo**	4
"Curly Doodle"	**Beth Glick**	13
"The Juggler of Day Is Gone"	**Nancy Lang Boyer**	20
"FARM"	**Jillian Wright Prout**	22
"Broken Wing"	**Jillian Wright Prout**	26
"Female Eider Duck"	**Wesley Bahorik**	29
"Spirit Doodle"	**Beth Glick**	30
"Sacred Dance"	**Rev. Michael Barnett**	32
"Loud Bouquet"	**Marilyn Basehoar**	34
"Fold Illusion Doodle"	**Beth Glick**	36
"Lady Birdbrain"	**Dr. Jill Beech**	38
"Apostrophe Doodle"	**Beth Glick**	40
"Intense Doodle"	**Beth Glick**	43
"We Dance"	**Krysta Bernhardt**	44
"The Band"	**Albert Ciervo**	47
"Who Are These People"	**Deborah Maguire Meehan**	48
"Club"	**Albert Ciervo**	50
"Peaceful Knowing"	**Kathryn E. Noska**	52
"Eat Alotta Peaches"	**Susan Biebuyck**	54
"Explosion"	**Kimberlee Dawn**	56
"Gougane Barra"	**Barrie Maguire**	58
"Floor Moss"	**Barrie Maguire**	61
"Rose on the Grey"	**Ivy Egger**	62
"Favorites"	**Suzanne Fellows**	64
"My Mother's Picture"	**Jennifer Gittings-Dalton**	66
"Peacock Doodle"	**Beth Glick**	69
" The Hopes of Daybreak"	**Wendy Fox**	70
"Petal Perfect"	**Wendy Fox**	73
"White Oak"	**Walt Hug**	74
"Reflection of the Mind"	**Joanne Moy**	76
"Winds of Change"	**Steve Fabian**	78
"Peeper on the Window"	**Susan Biebuyck**	80
"Wisdom"	**Lauralynn White**	84
"Listening for Harmony"	**Kathryn E. Noska**	86

Title	Author	Page
"Untitled"	Ron Schira	89
"The Pollinator Prayer"	Victoria Lawrence	90
"Pomona and Vertumnus'	Victoria Lawrence	93
"Blooms Stand Tall"	Lisa Mitchell	94
"Tony & Joe"	Jim Meehan	96
"Just a Guy on the Phone '	Jim Meehan	101
"Languor"	Lauralynn White	102
"A Walk in the Woods"	Nancy Lang Boyer	105
"Music of the Stones"	Bob Hakun	106
"Twig Bird"	Bob Hakun	109
"Family Guy"	Deborah Maguire Meehan	110
"Spotlight"	Hilary Swingle	114
"Sing-Along"	Marianne Buschini	116
"For You"	Merrill Weber	118
"Relinquish"	Lauralynn White	121
"Veranda View"	Merrill Weber	122
"Standards of Beauty"	Angela Izzo	124
"Ice Bubble II"	Rachel Conrad	126
"Denise"	Amanda Condict	128
"Leg Drawings"	Anne Chase	130
"Fred"	Amanda Condict	132
"The Celebrator"	Hilary Swingle	134
"In the Balance"	Kathryn E. Noska	140
"Koi Pond"	Marilyn Fox	142
"A Road Less Traveled"	Nicole Johnson	145
"Untitled"	Ron Schira	146
"Vesuvius, 2021"	Daniella Yacono	148
"ART"	Jerry Kott	151
"Winding Tree"	Anne Chase	152
"Treescape" acrylic	Joanne Moy	154
"Bear Fever Puzzle"		156
"Nightshade Hunter-Gatherer"	Bob Hakun	161
"Girls Club"	Maryanne Buschini	162
"Doodle Floral"	Beth Glick	165
"TRUTH"	Jerry Kott	166
"Leg Drawings"	Anne Chase	170
"Untitled"	Ron Schira	172

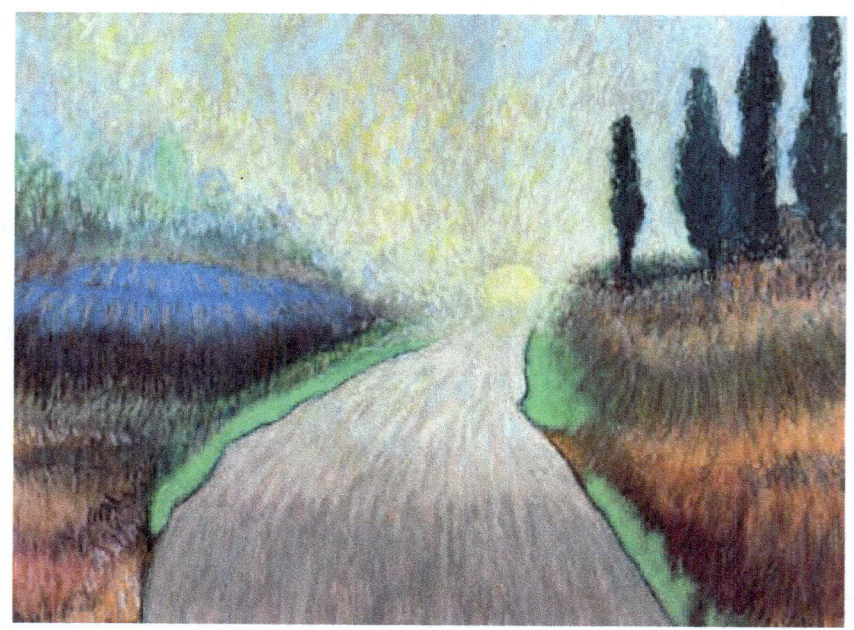

"The Juggler of Day Is Gone" pastel *Nancy Lang Boyer*

NANCY LANG BOYER

Dedication

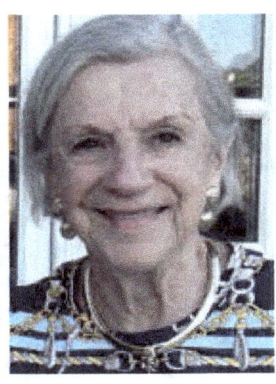

"My Favorite Things," Studio B's 8th book of poetry, prose, and art is dedicated to *Nancy Lang Boyer*, one of Studio B Fine Art Gallery's most loyal patrons, known fondly as the "First Lady of Boyertown." Nancy left us on December 17, 2020, at the age of 94.

"'The Juggler of Day Is Gone' based on an Emily Dickinson poem of the same title. Mom loved Emily Dickinson and this was the only painting she did after my dad died in 1990. My husband Chris Hall noticed it at a Retrospective of her work years later and contacted the woman who owned the painting by offering to buy it from her. (He did not say he was Nancy's son-in-law.) She declined. He then offered more. She declined. He offered even more to purchase it and she declined. So I asked my mom to paint another one -- and it was the only painting that she made a copy of." ~ *Mary Ann Boyer*

THE JUGGLER OF DAY

Emily Dickinson

Blazing in gold and quenching in purple,
Leaping like leopards to the sky,
Then at the feet of the old horizon
Laying her spotted face, to die;

Stooping as low as the otter's window,
Touching the roof and tinting the barn,
Kissing her bonnet to the meadow,
And the juggler of day is gone!

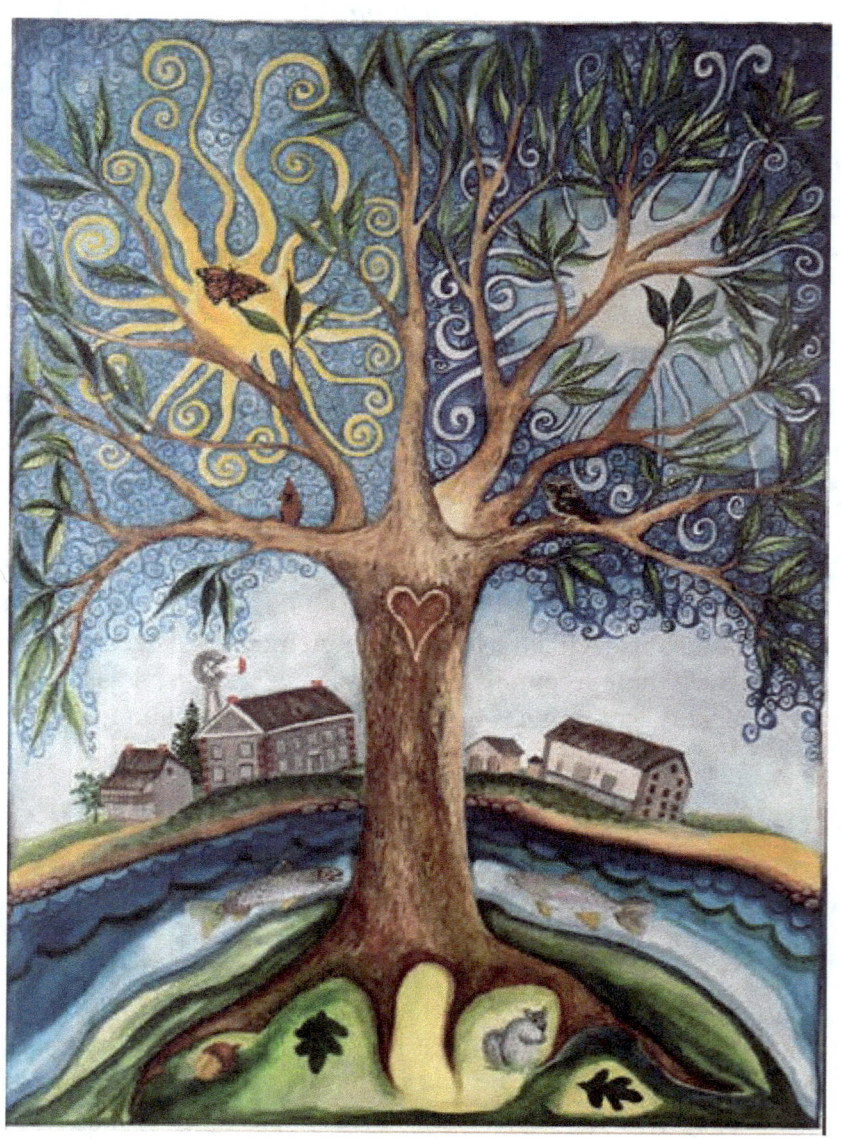

"FARM" watercolor — *Jillian Wright Prout*

The True Meaning of "Farm"
~ Claudia Bahorik

To a shy kid from the country, first grade started out being some of the worst of times. First grade, in retrospect, would also be responsible for some of the best of times. It was a year full of memories that still live even some seventy years later, and still bring a smile to my face. Many of these memories might explain why I am what I have become, or once had been.

First grade was when I finally was able to ride that big yellow bus along with my big brother. It was also when I discovered that I could not wear my bibbed overalls to school, and I had to wear a "damn dress" (that's what I told my mother, and not to her delight – although she did crack a wicked smile when she told my father).

It was in first grade that I learned the difference between cruelty and kindness. I was a naive five when I happily hopped on that yellow bus, only to discover my brother had suddenly disowned me. There I sat in that damn dress, lunch box clutched to my heart in protective mode, wondering if I would ever survive the bus ride with those taunting older kids (apparently, they didn't like my dress either). That moment probably was when the seeds for hating school were first sown.

My next memory was one of abject terror. Getting off that bus that was parked helter-skelter among a sea of yellow, dotted with swarms of kids. Kids smiling, talking to friends, all seeming to know where to go next. Everyone smiling but me. Fear and loneliness found a home in my heart that first day. It was the day I discovered, in general, no one gave a damn about one lost kid.

My second memory of first grade was sitting in the middle of a class of kids, all of which were strangers, and looking down at my shoe that had become untied. The teacher had already established her position as a disciplinarian and as one that a skinny, scared first-grader could not even dream of running to with any type of kiddie crisis. The more I looked at the untied shoe, and listened to the chalk scraping on the blackboard, the more I withdrew. I feared the bell for recess, because it would be then that she and the other kids discovered I couldn't tie my shoes. It would be then that more teasing would resume.

The dreaded bell rang, and tears rolled down in panicked silence. I sat there still looking down at my untied lace. And then came the miracle. Mark, the only kid I now recall was in that miserable first grade class, bent over and tied my shoe. It was then that I realized in that swarm of blank faces, there was someone who was kind and cared. I think that was the only time I remember smiling and being happy in first grade. Thank you, Mark.

Of course, happiness was short-lived in the mind of a first grader that had difficulty saying words with the letter, "L." Our battle-axe teacher, her name forever repressed, had a nasty habit of separating us kids into reading groups. She took pleasure in announcing to the class which group was full of dummies. That was the group someone who barely knew the alphabet and could not say "L" was always stuck in.

Unfortunately, old Mrs. Battle-axe took pleasure in humiliating students who didn't live up to her rigid expectations. If a kid had problems reading out loud, that was the kid she would make stand up and read in front of the entire class of laughing eyes. That's how I viewed it the day she picked me to read.

I stood quivering in one of those damn dresses, underarms dripping, slowly trying to read without her admonishment. I came to the word, "farm." That was not an "L" word, but I had never seen it before. I lived on a farm, but never had to spell it.

I paused. Battle-axe loudly announced, "farm!" I continued reading and came to "farm" again. I couldn't remember what it was. Too many eyes staring at me. She snapped louder, "Farm!!" I read on. By Jesus, that word "farm" appeared a third time. By then, the mental block was solidified. Old Battle-axe slammed the book down and screamed, "FARM!!!"

The next thing I remember about the word "farm," was sitting under my desk, shaking and crying, and wetting my pants. I never had done anything so embarrassing before. I recall nothing else about first grade. Not what happened, not the bus ride home, not what my mother said. I only remember hating to read from that day forward. Sadly, the only real thing that made me smile like a bird discovering wings, was the day I opened my report card and saw I had "passed" first grade. That was to be remembered as the second miracle of my young life.

It wasn't until third grade that lessons learned in first grade, including my hatred of reading and school in general, began to be overcome. I had become accustomed to those damn dresses that inhibited my play during recess. My teacher, Mrs. Dauber, seemed to never notice me, at least she never humiliated me and didn't make me read aloud.

Then it happened. I became deathly ill and landed in the hospital. A month later I returned home, weak and not able to return to school. This time I cried to my mother, that I was afraid that missing so much school would cause me to flunk. I had been humiliated enough and I feared the stigma of being held back.

Then the third miracle happened. Mrs. Dauber showed up at our door one evening. I recall being tucked in blankets, lying on my "sick bed" on the sofa, and her sitting down next to me. I had never noticed her smile before, and surely, never knew she cared. She brought homework for me and told me not to worry about failing. It was the first of several visits. She brought me books, a sense of feeling cared for, and most of all, she gave me hope.

Because of Mrs. Dauber taking me under her wing, and helping me to read and pass third grade, I gained the confidence to persist in the face of adversity. She also helped me smile when I returned to school. Sure, there were other teachers who helped draw the shy, skinny country bumpkin out of her shell. But it was my third-grade teacher who gave me the wings to fly. Thank you, Mrs. Dauber.

I am now a retired family practice physician who, among other achievements, can say the letter "L" and sure as hell knows the word "farm!"

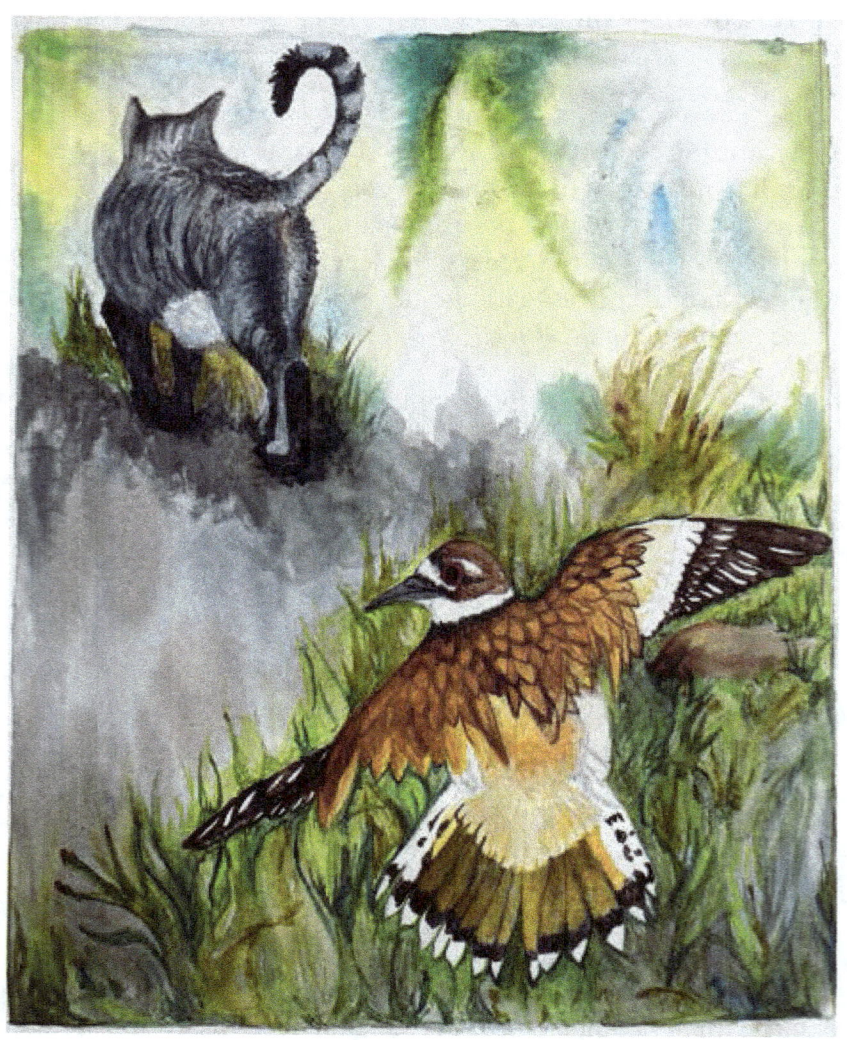

"Broken Wing" watercolor　　　　　　　　*Jillian Wright Prout*

WHAT MAKES ME HAPPY
~ J. Wesley Bahorik, Ph.D.

We humans have been well indoctrinated to believe non-human animals don't or can't think; don't have feelings and motivations; don't have senses like intention, responsibility, concern; nor do they have the ability for complex problem solving. What makes me happy is when I experience or hear of occasions when nature proves us wrong!

I recall an incident involving a bird, a killdeer, solving a number of problems while protecting its nest. On this occasion, I was grooming a horse in a paddock in front of our barn when a killdeer flew into the paddock, landed not more than eight feet from me, and began flopping and thrashing about like it was seriously injured. This behavior has been called the "broken wing act" and is employed by the killdeer when it fears some danger is approaching its nest or young. The bird pretends to be disabled to distract some predator.

Since killdeer will construct a nest of hollowed out dirt and pebbles on open ground, I assumed there was a nest nearby in the paddock area near me. I stopped grooming the horse and turned to watch the antics of the bird. It thrashed about a few moments then flew away. The act of flying away a short distance is part of the act to mislead unwanted visitors. I looked briefly to see the nest but couldn't find it, went back to grooming the horse when, suddenly, the bird reappeared, flopped back onto the ground a few feet away, thrashed about as though it was wounded. Again, it flew off in the direction of a lane leading to our lower pasture, flopped down on the ground again but further down the lane.

By now, the bird had my attention. I began to think it wanted me to follow, as it repeated the broken wing act each time that I made an attempt to approach. This charade continued down the lane for about 100 yards until I spotted a rather portly house cat at the lower end of the lane. As soon as the cat saw me approaching, it took off at a dead run, its mad dash appearing like the cat had seen the devil himself or some hideous monster from outer space. The cat's frantic dash into the woodlot and away from me and the killdeer brought a smile to my face. It was a happy thought that my presence probably saved the killdeer's nest and young.

My feelings of pleasure at seeing the cat wildly fleeing began to amplify when I realized what the bird had done. The killdeer must have realized it was no match for the cat near its nest and needed help. It must have seen me in the paddock and figured the cat would be no match for me. It surely must have calculated the capabilities of both me and the cat and knew I could be of service to get rid of the menace. Then it solved the problem of the distance between me and the cat by flying into the paddock to perform the broken wing act. As soon as I responded by moving toward the bird, it continued the act, each time moving farther down the lane and closer to the cat. When the cat fled in a panic, the bird also disappeared and no longer came back. It must have reasoned I was no longer needed, the cat was gone, and my role could easily change from savior to predator.

I did not look for the nest for fear I might step on the camouflaged depression in the ground, I never saw the cat again, the killdeer made no more appearances that day, and I went back to grooming the horse with a warm sense of satisfaction. My respect for the problem-solving capabilities of a killdeer was greatly enhanced. For me, happiness isn't always jumping up and down for joy. My happiness in this case was the profound thought that nature had once again proven humans and their anthropomorphic set of values can be quite wrong.

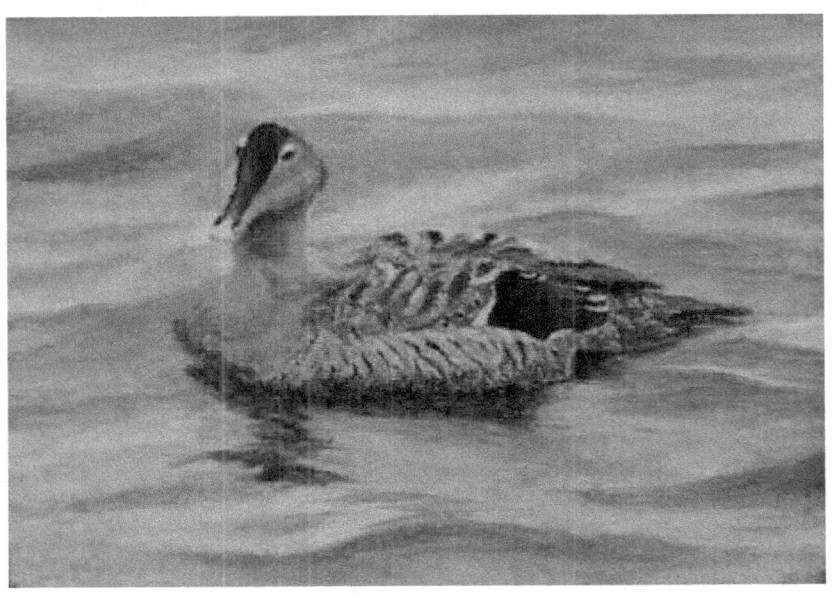

"Female Eider Duck" acrylic   *Wesley Bahorik*

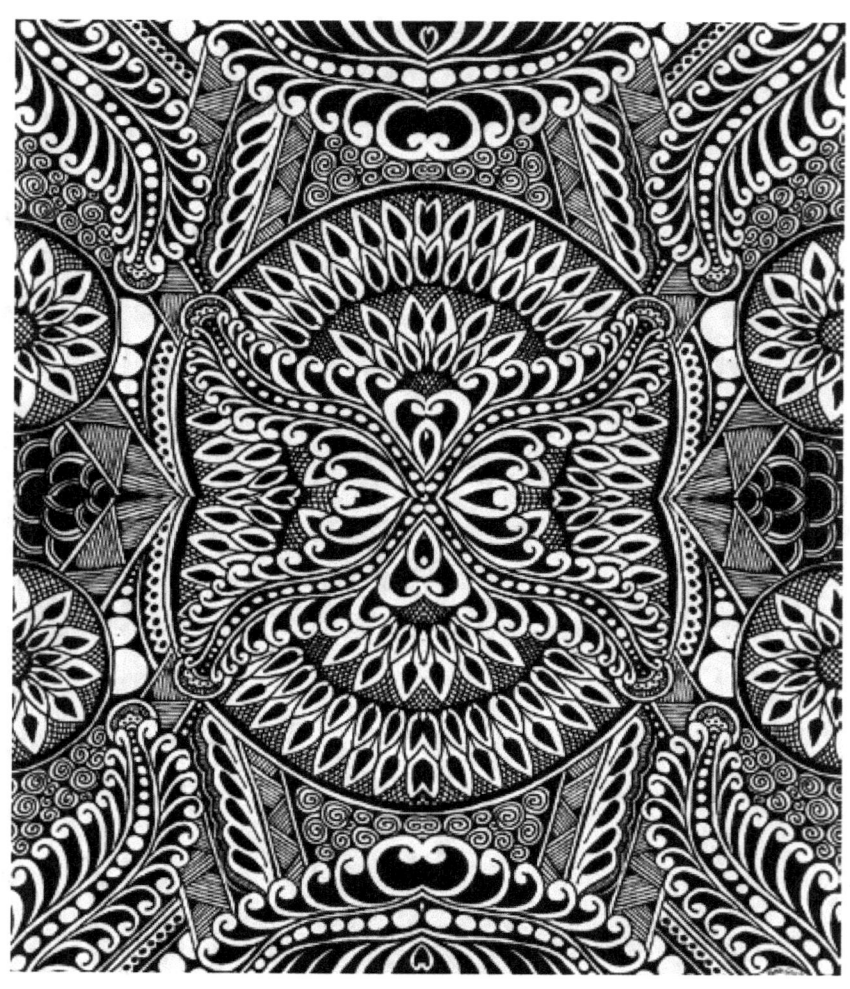

"Spirit Doodle" ink   **Beth Glick**

My Favorite Things: Leading Guided Meditations

~ Rev. Michael Barnett, M, Div., M.Ed.

After many years offering Blue Turtle Intuitive Tarot sessions, Spirit told me to "get ready for small group work" during a day of readings at the Ark spiritual bookstore in Santa Fe, New Mexico, one summer 7 years ago. I had no idea how this would begin, but I always surrender in total trust to Spirit and shared this information with my clients and people who attended my intuitive classes at Souderton Area Community Education and workshops at Earth-Speak in Kimberton and at the Ark in Santa Fe.

Lo and behold! Two groups of people came forward to start two small intuitive groups meeting monthly during the academic year in Lansdale and Douglassville, Berks County. What began grew into the Blue Turtle Mystery School of Emerging Eternity where I would call upon the healing energies to come forth to guide, lead, and protect us in our spiritual work supporting one another's development and growth with Spirit.

Over the years, what actually happened was that I regularly facilitated as an instrument of Spirit the presence of different sacred beings pertinent to our intuitive work together to come forth and speak to us, bless us, and anoint and replenish us as we grew in our gifts and served others in the world in various capacities.

It was remarkable that we grew together and were blessed by the presence, guidance, and protection of these sacred beings. Our Mystery School and intuitive classes continue in safe ways during this pandemic as we continue to help one another and serve others in our communities and lives as instruments of the Divine. I surrendered once again trusting Spirit completely, working with the people whom I can serve in this sacred way.

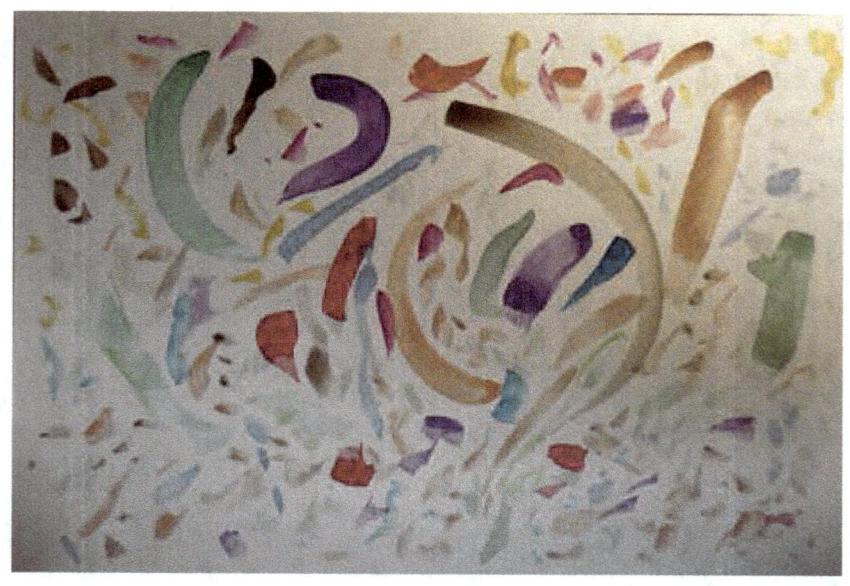

"Sacred Dance" watercolor   **Rev. Michael Barnett**

My Favorite Things: Making Vibrational Healing Art

~ Rev. Michael Barnett, M, Div., M.Ed.

One of my favorite things as part of my Blue Turtle Intuitive Counseling work is making vibrational healing art. Initially, when I began my spiritual work reading intuitive tarot cards as an instrument of Spirit in 1988 in Northern Liberties, Philadelphia, PA, where I lived in neighborhood and community fairs on weekends, I was guided by Spirit to also offer vibrational healing art cards.

When I created these cards, I would come from that sacred place within where I would connect with the Divine energy through my Intuitive Self and receive the dancing, colorful energies that would take me spontaneously, "perfectly," from color to card, back and forth, until the art was done. I was a conduit of the sacred energy. The general, abstract, dancing, color energies placed upon the card would contain the healing colors, forms, and energies that would enhance and support the person drawn to it in her life.

People were so moved by these powerful, sustaining cards that they "tuned-in" and bought for themselves, their loved ones, and friends the vibrational healing art cards which resonated intuitively with them. Over time, my vibrational healing art cards were in card shops and spiritual shops in Pennsylvania, New Mexico, and Ontario, Canada, where I travelled and lived.

After many years, Spirit encouraged me to expand the cards into smaller and larger vibrational healing art paintings. I was asked to make vibrational healing art cards and paintings for people "tuning-into" specific people in their lives. I sold cards and paintings at regional spiritual expos in New Mexico, Pennsylvania, and New Jersey where I also did readings and programs.

I have given gifts of these vibrational healing art cards and paintings to people in my life who remark, "I cannot believe that you've captured my favorite colors which I wear and love around me. I feel the healing energies." I began using watercolors and have moved into acrylics as well. I love offering these cards and paintings to support and help people as part of my Blue Turtle Intuitive Counseling work.

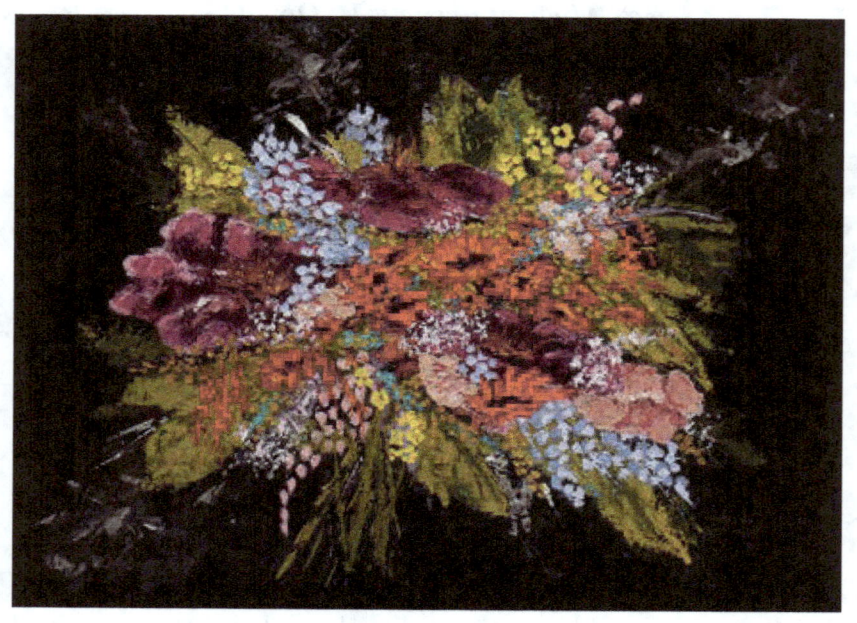

"Loud Bouquet" *acrylic*   ***Marilyn Basehoar***

The Loud Bouquet

~ *Marilyn Basehoar*

We danced in the early morning sunshine,
    Wearing our brightest dresses.

We swayed in the afternoon breeze,
    Shouting out our glory.

We showed off in the quiet evening,
    Celebrating our sparkling colors.

We lit up the starry night skies,
    Resplendent in our neon gowns.

Look! We shouted. Look at us!
    We are all dressed up, if only you will look.

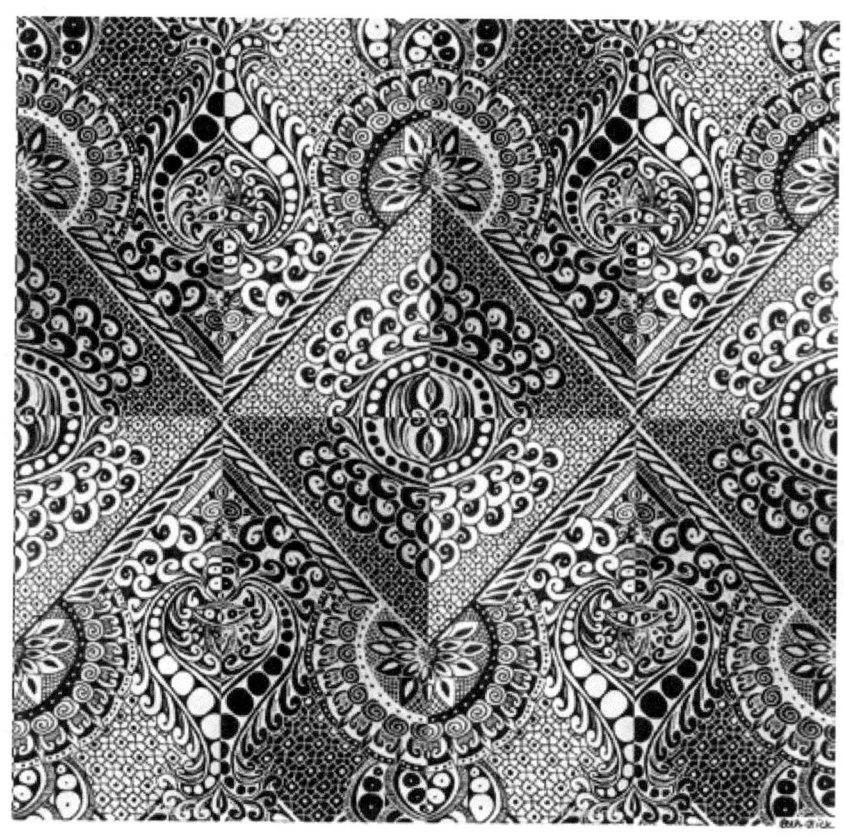

"Fold Illusion Doodle" ink   **Beth Glick**

INSIDE THE KALEIDOSCOPE
~ *Virginia Beards*

Inside this thing, tunnel-vision fragments swirl
and random chips of joy and stress collide.
At the slightest turn a still world starts to spin.

Red, blue and yellow bits overlap, refract—
   a mandala with no center, a café somewhere

      a red bedroom, a white Matisse dove
         infinitely spooling lines of black ink

         spindrift and foam-blow in an open boat
            scents of a stable, muck of a farm pond.

               Death: the dwindling hiss of an espresso machine
                  the tallyho of a distant troll.

Slammed by spinning images and shiny shards,
I peer through Sir David Brewster's curious device—
in every twist, a riff of yes, or no, or if, or why,
and the allure of chaos morphing into form.

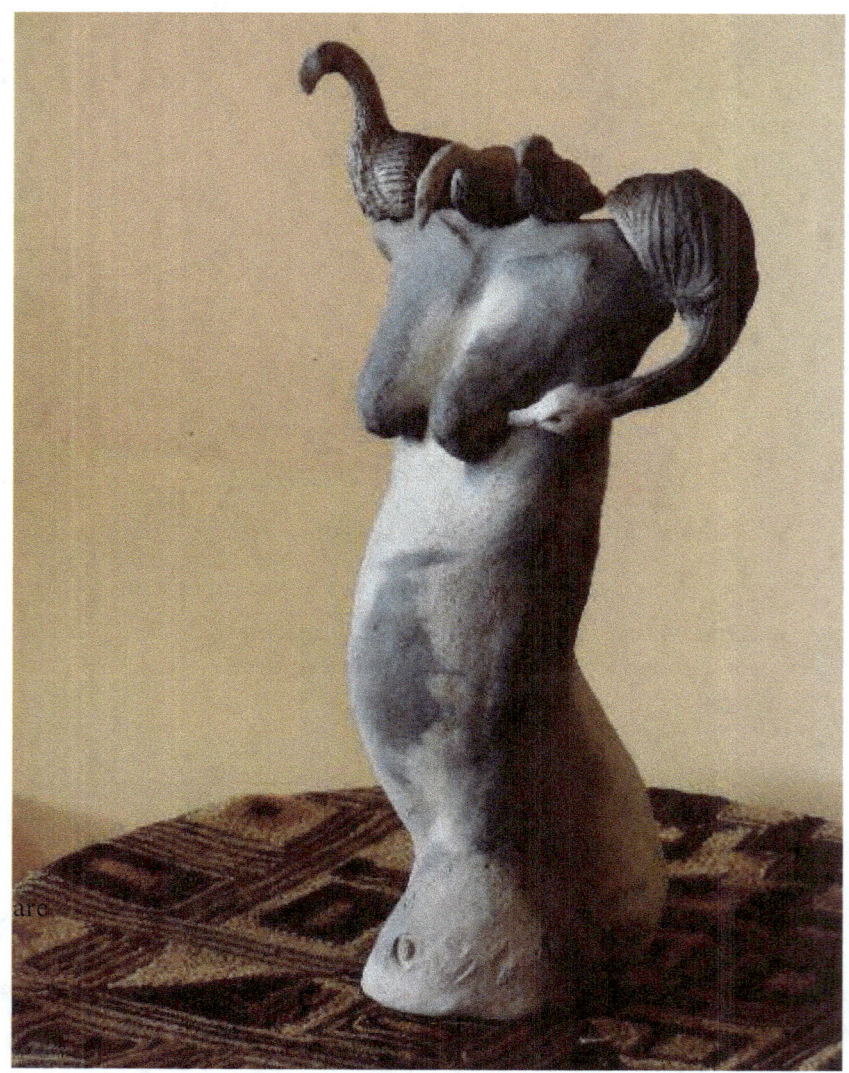

"Lady Birdbrain" sculpture — **Dr. Jill Beech**

The Lady Birdbrain Sculpture
~ *Virginia Beards*

Her torso stops where her neck should start,
she has no head. Birds erupt from her rotator cuffs,
burst out of her clavicles—ascend, flutter,
blink and gaze.

Today Lady Birdbrain's a pelican,
neck cocked, she listens.
Catch a fish, catch an indiscretion?
Queen of upward soar and downward surge.
Occasionally, her breast turns red
and she appears to vomit.

Sometimes she molts into goosebrain,
sits and fusses, natters and clucks
among her flock at Starbucks.
"A common feature in the urban environment,"
so notes *The Guide to North American Birding*.

Lady Birdbrain channels raven.
Swoosh, she's an airborne Proteus
with obsidian eye and ebony cape.
Shape shifter, shifty trickster,
Deliverer, provider, protector.
Lady. Bird. Brain.

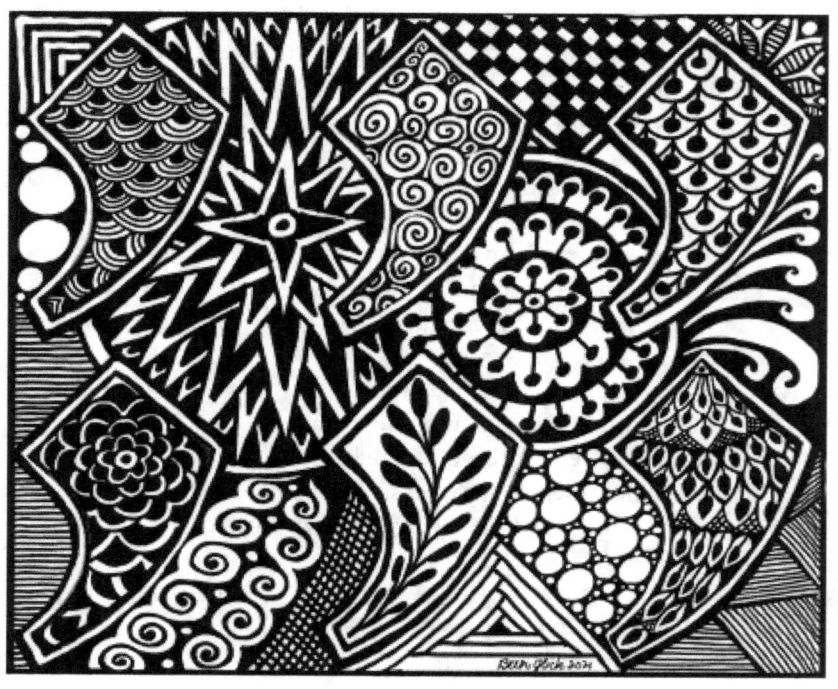

"Apostrophe Doodle" ink   **Beth Glick**

THE MYTH OF APOSTROPHES
~Craig Bennett

I've always loved mythology. The ancient world of gods and goddesses is a source of endless fascination for me, and myths often explain so much that would otherwise remain a mystery. For example, we've all heard of at least some of the gods and heroes of ancient Greek mythology. Hercules, Pericles, Achilles, Socrates, and Euripides are just a few of the better-known. But how many of us are familiar with Apostrophes, the ancient Greek god of punctuation?

Now, Apostrophes was a Titan, a being sort of half-way between gods and humans. Actually, the mighty Zeus had created a variety of races when he created the world. In addition to the Titans, there was the race of gold, the race of silver, and the race of bronze. But Zeus was dissatisfied with each of these three creations, so he destroyed each of them in its turn. Finally, he created the race of iron, which is our own—the human race.

Life was not easy for the iron race. They had to struggle for everything they gained, and their material existence was a meager one. When they invented writing, for example, they had no punctuation. All the words ran together in one huge block, and there was no telling where one idea stopped and another began, or which groups of words were there only to tell something about another group, or what words the author wrote as opposed to those of someone else whose words he was merely quoting. It was so difficult to make clear and logical sense of anything someone wrote that it was almost as bad as having no writing at all.

Apostrophes looked down on this predicament from the slopes of Mount Olympus (only the gods could afford to live at the very top) and felt pity for poor, suffering human beings. Out of his compassion he resolved to do something to make life in general—and reading in particular—less trying for the miserable race of iron. He resolved that he would defy the very gods themselves and give the gift of punctuation to humans.

That night he grabbed a roomy sack and ascended the rest of the way to the very top of Mount Olympus. Though everything was shrouded in darkness, he knew exactly where he wanted to go: to the offices of the *Weekly Olympian*, the newsletter of the gods. Groping his way through the murky streets, he finally arrived at the building and gained entrance through a ground-floor window. Once inside, he was able to locate the main press room and the all-important type bins. He opened his sack and quickly began scooping up handfuls of commas, periods, semicolons — every punctuation mark he could find — and dropping them in.

Once he had finished, he hurried down the mountainside to the Earth below, where the dismal race of iron were still trying to make out what each other had written. When the mighty Titan reached into his sack and began to distribute punctuation marks, the race of iron went nearly mad with joy and gratitude. "We can read!" they exclaimed. "We can *understand*!"

Apostrophes stood back and smiled with a sort of paternal satisfaction. He was glad he had done this thing, and it warmed his heart to see the ecstatic expression of long-awaited comprehension on the faces of men and women. But he knew there would be a price to pay. One didn't defy the gods of Olympus and expect to get away with it.

Sure enough, when the gods found out what Apostrophes had done, they were plenty miffed. "That miserable twit!" grumbled Zeus. "I'll fix his wagon — *big time*!"

So, Apostrophes, the mighty Titan, was captured, bound, and taken to a high precipice in the far-off mountains of the Caucasus. There he was chained to a blackboard for all eternity; and every day, an old professor emeritus would come and read to him in a monotone, hour after hour, from annotated commentaries on the works of John Donne and Edmund Spenser. It was a *horrible* punishment. But Apostrophes knew that he had made a worthy sacrifice and that he had the everlasting gratitude of humankind. They were so grateful, in fact, that they gave his name to one of the punctuation marks that he had brought from the cloudy heights of Mount Olympus. And that, so the story goes, is how we came to have apostrophes.

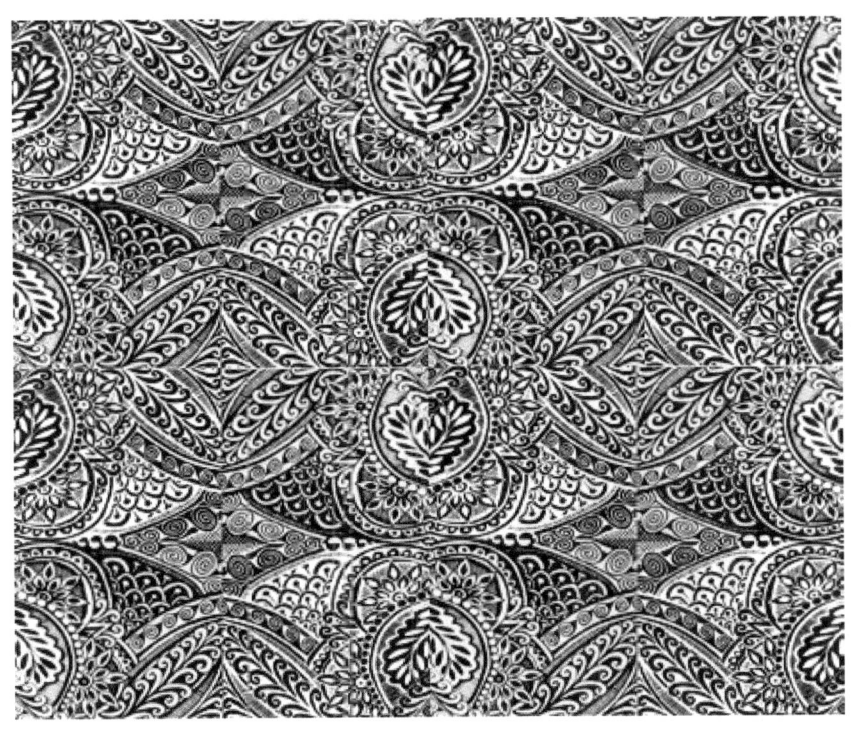

"Intense Doodle" ink   **Beth Glick**

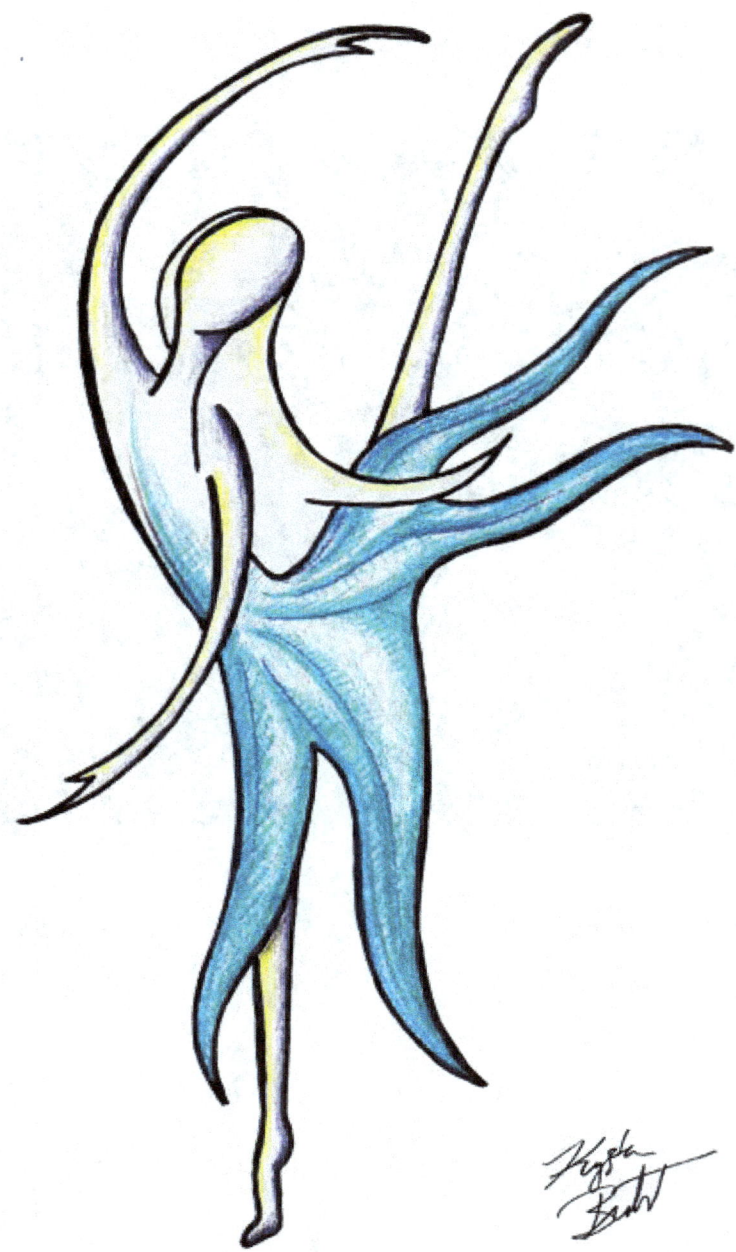

"We Dance" mixed media — Krysta Bernhardt

WE DANCE

~ *Krysta Bernhardt*

Once a week I take a ballet class. It's for grownups. It's hard to find dance classes for grownups. There are so many of us that used to dance. As young girls, it was almost expected that we dance, but as grown women it is expected that we stop. It is generally assumed that we are no longer able or that we are not worthy of watching anymore.

When you are a young girl, youth, beauty and grace are almost synonymous with donning a tutu and taking to the stage. As a grown woman, unless you are a professional, not so much. When I started dancing again a few years ago after about a 15-year break, I got rolled eyes and sniggers from more than a few less-than-understanding people.

The class is taught by a small, limber, older woman. I don't know her age. Her grace and passion for what she teaches make it difficult to tell just how old she is. (And really – who cares anyway?)

As the classes begin each week, our bodies creak and crack and moan. Our legs, which once raised above our waists now hover at 45 degrees on a good day. Our feet, which once turned out so easily, are encumbered by rickety hips that complain a lot more than they used to. Our shoulders catch and our backs aren't as flexible, but each week we come to class and we work and we sweat. Each week we stretch and we strengthen and we move.

On the surface, maybe it seems silly. I have certainly gotten that reaction from people. Why would middle-aged moms and grandmoms want to don leotards and prance around in front of the mirror every week? Maybe people think we are trying to recapture a lost chapter of our lives.

Today's world is so uber focused on the beauty of being young. Being physically beautiful when you are young is easy. It is so difficult to maintain a sense of beauty about yourself as you age. Your legs aren't as smooth as they used to be. Your face is weathered and your belly is soft from having babies. In today's world, physical beauty is valued above all else. As you age and these things slip away, it is too easy to feel that your place in the world no longer has any worth. It's too easy to stop trying because society thinks that you are invisible or that what you have to offer doesn't matter.

But in that room, even though our legs don't stretch as high and even though our backs don't curve like they used to, there is a strength and beauty and grace that didn't exist when we were young girls. We have seen. We have done. We have birthed. We have cared for. We have lost people. We have experienced life. We are women.

So each week we show up. Each week we persist. Each week we come back, and we stretch, and as the music starts, it's not about recapturing our lost youth. It's not about staving off inevitable old age. It's about moving, and feeling, and dancing and being. It's about celebrating the women we are and the women we are becoming.

We dance. We dance for ourselves, we dance for each other, we dance for our children and our families and our lives. We dance for the past we once knew, for the now, and the future we are creating

We dance, and it's a beautiful thing.

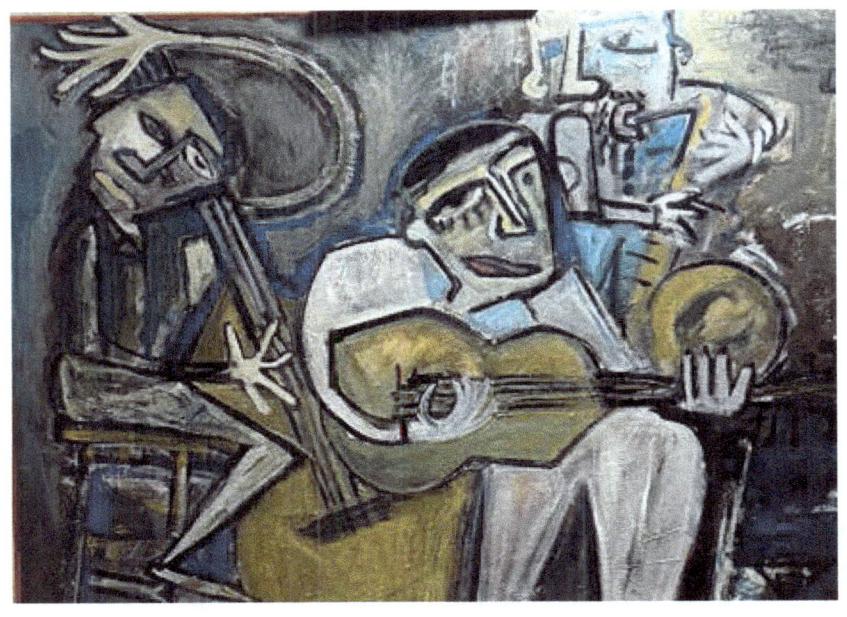

"The Band" acrylic   *Albert Ciervo*

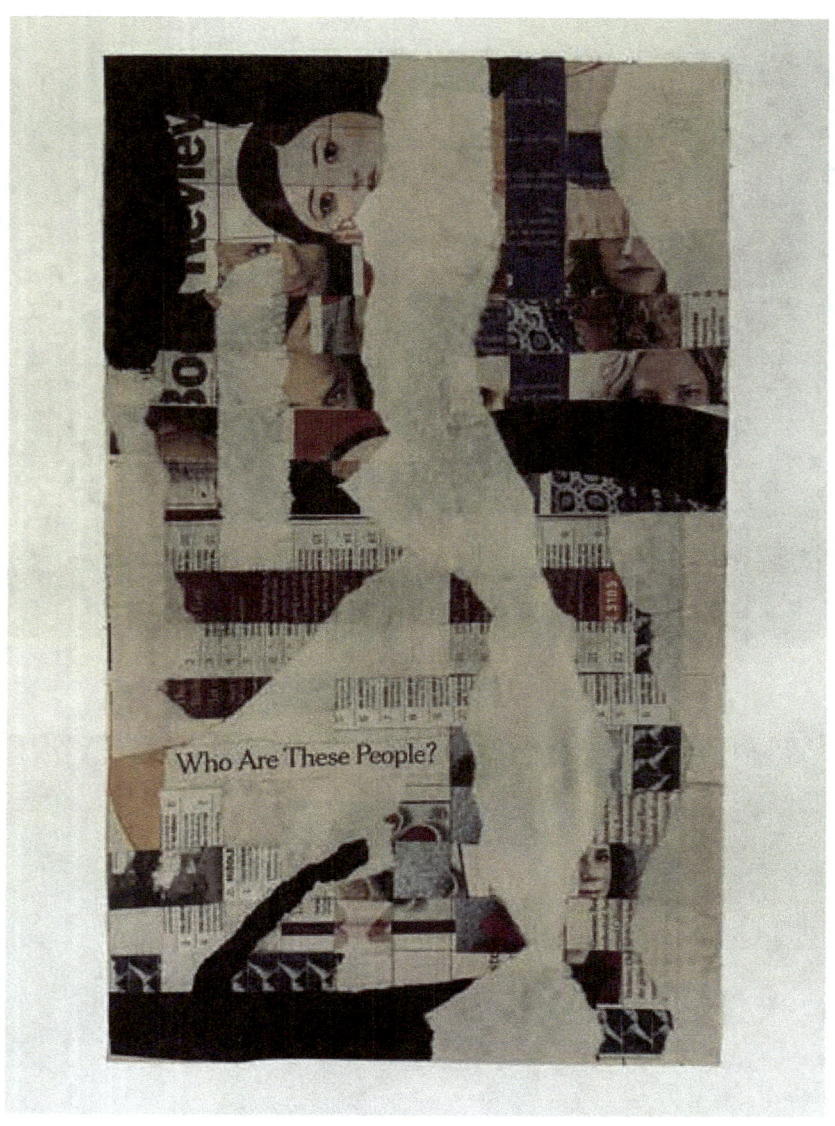

"Who Are These People" collage   **Deborah Maguire Meehan**

Forgotten

~Cathryn Clinton

Your touch
pervades
the amnesia
with tangible.

Now you
are memory:
of summer
on lips,
silk,
in skin,
breath
of deep,
rhythm.

My soul
discerns sensate
even in
separateness.

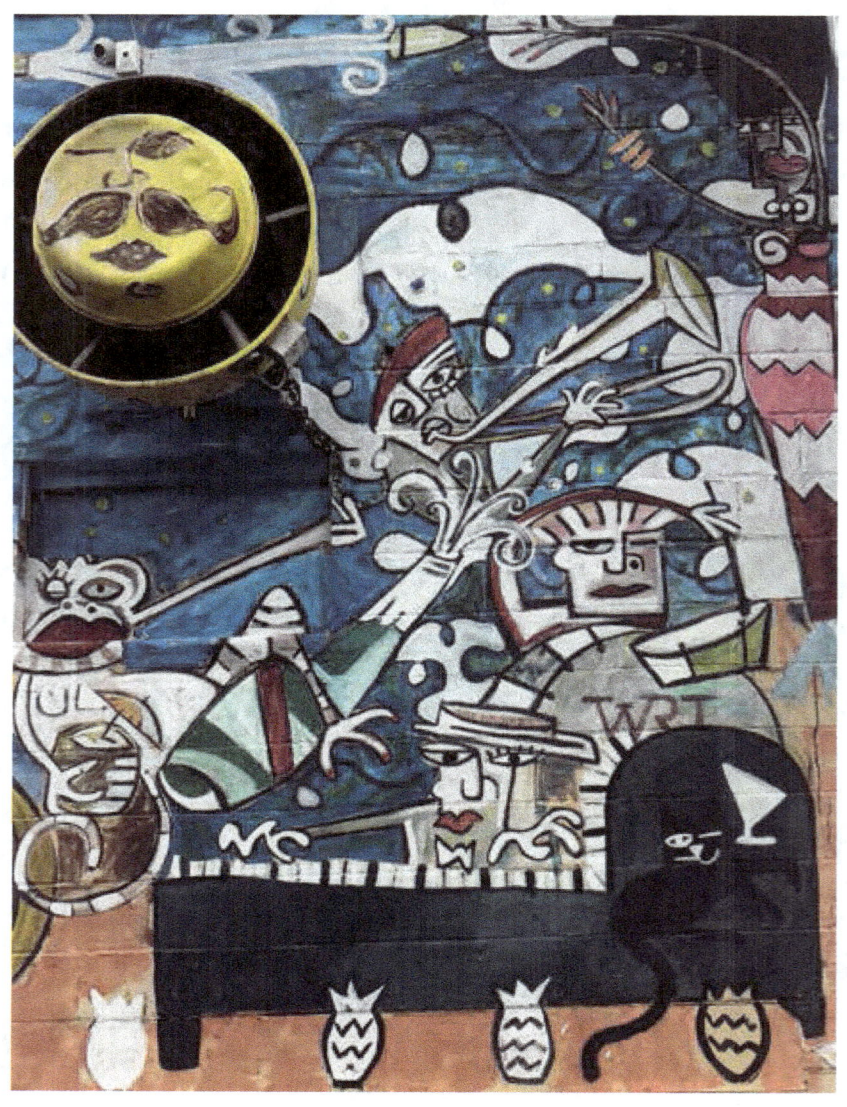

"Club" mural   **Albert Ciervo**

DAYCLUB

~ *Tony Cocuzza*

I am not asking for much
All I want is a Nightclub that is open in the daytime
on a Tuesday or a Thursday in the middle of the morning
an escape from Hellish heat, merciless cold, and the World's annoying routines
Maybe it will offer moving flesh and limbs or moving Music - Anything that can move me
I would be admired for the density of my Personality - Not the thickness of my wallet
This Dayclub would serve perpetual Pancakes and sell Cat Food
I would wear one of my favorite shirts and my lucky underwear
Is this not the Land of Opportunity and the sometimes Free?
I am not asking for much
I want to exit this Club in early afternoon, self-smitten by this dizzy Half-life
Cat Food tucked under my arm; Maple Syrup lingering on my lips

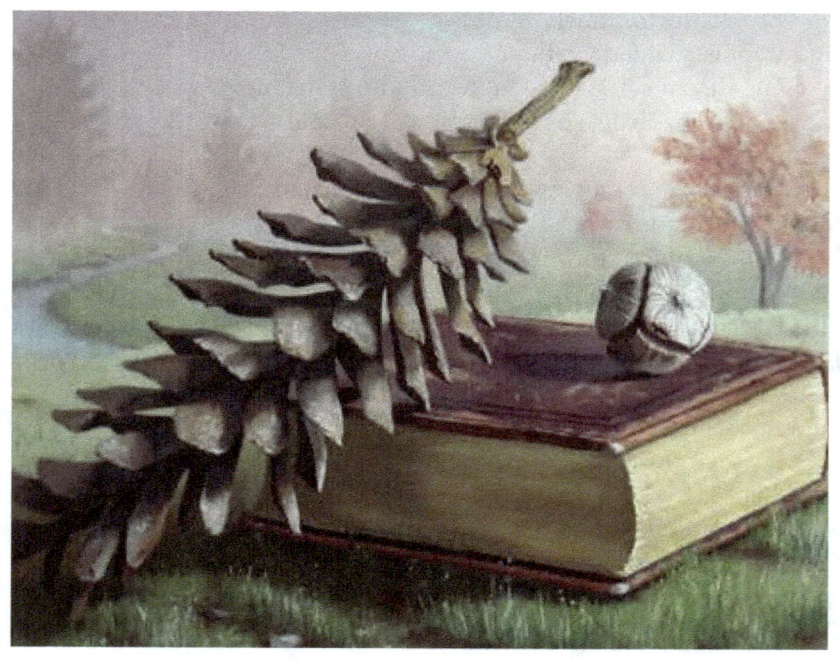

"Peaceful Knowing" oil   *Kathryn E. Noska*

SAVED

~Tony Cocuzza

Books on my crowded shelf
I should read them a second time
to see if they disrupt a different part of me
or give them to someone in need of disruption
I allow my favorite music to collect cobwebs of neglect
so I may avoid their bittersweet gateway to Truth or Speculation
I seldom wear my favorite shirts
only as a shield against discord and joyless ritual
Why am I saving them?
There are lonely food items in my pantry
patiently awaiting the onslaught of insects or expiration date
Candles and Incense, still sealed, rehearsing for some fragrant occasion
Greeting cards and postcards immortalizing places I have barely seen
I should send them to those I have barely known
Why am I saving them?
I have spread myself thinly across many Worlds
Thinly - as a layer of Ice cracked, shattered by careless feet
I will offer something to one more World
Why am I saving it?

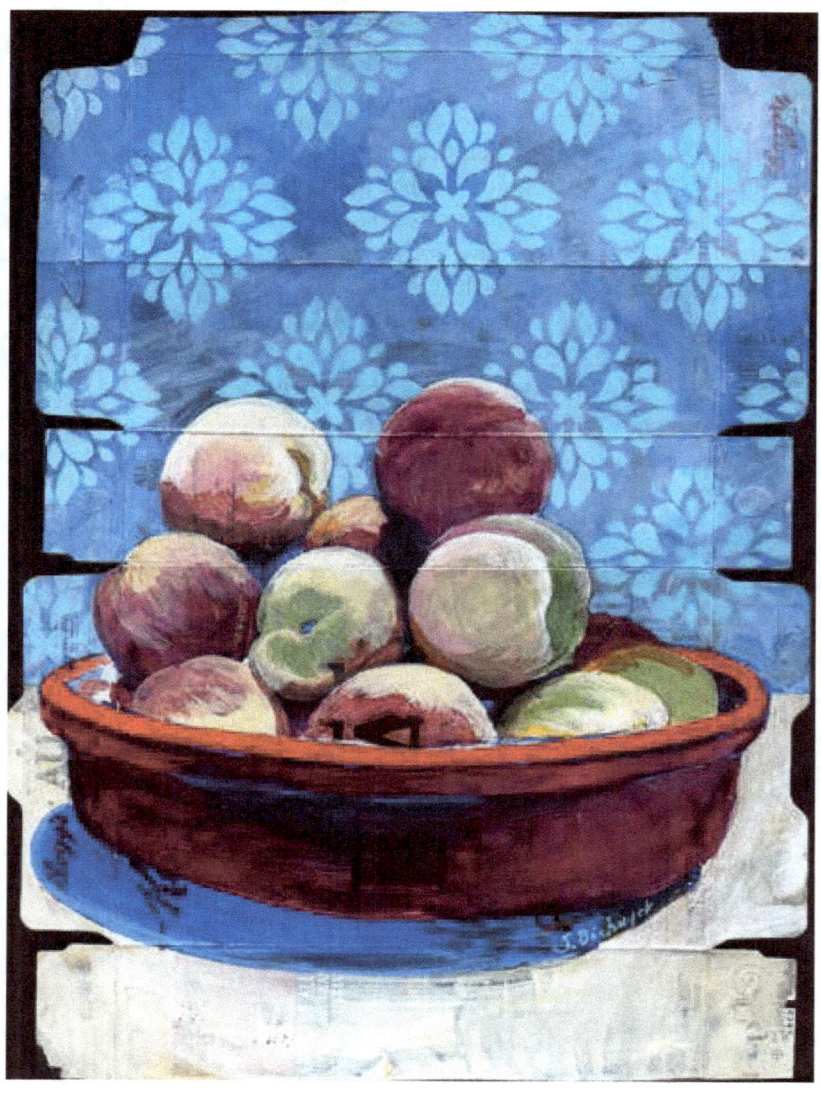

"Eat Alotta Peaches" oil on cereal box   **Susan Biebuyck**

Zerns Farmer's Market
early seventies

~ *Carole Croll*

It begins with peaches,
September's yield, peaches
from Zerns, the old Zerns.

(The Zerns with The Mighty
Atom, strongman, ancient and
bare-chested, lathering his beard

with edible soap, inviting
the crowd to take a swipe,
taste the goodness.) That Zerns.

Saturday night and it's time
to fold, pack up the stands
until next week. Farmers set

to go home empty, give away
whatever's left. Time to buy,
name a price, carry home

sweet bushels, summer's closing
scent. Monday morning after
blanching, grab a knife, peel

and halve. Fuzzy skins, en masse,
surrender stones with curious
etchings, clear, nothing left but

slippery flesh. Slice and pack,
looks like sunlight; sunrise, sunset
in a jar. All those meaty, mellow

peaches ready for a bath. Yes, it all
begins with peaches— syrup, lids
and twirling rings. Doesn't end

until the pop.

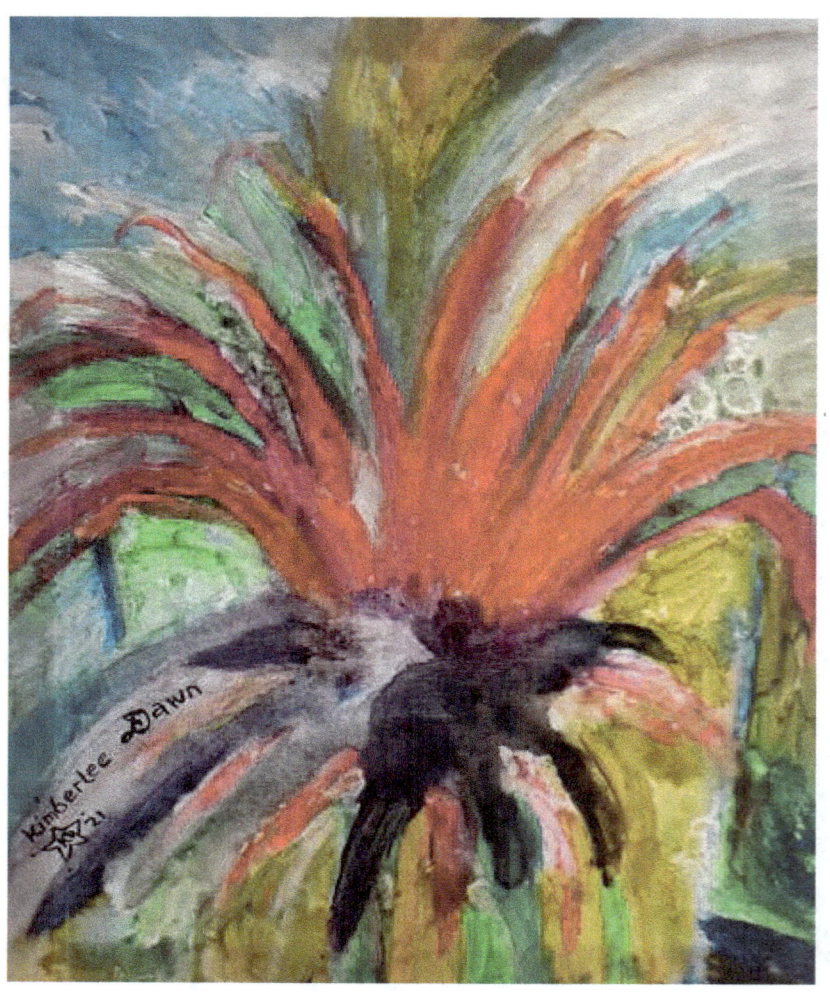

"Explosion" acrylic **Kimberlee Dawn**

BLESSED BEE BALM

~ *Kimberlee Dawn*

My beautiful red
headdresses of the
Native American, Black
African Chiefs…
Bee Balm
Explosion of color.

Sister photographs them
I paint them.
We wait all year for
their kingfisherness
Hello and welcome
Native Warriors
Red bright goddesses

Hello, my friends
from Oley
Now of the labyrinth
Native flowers
Bright, bold, watching

Bee balm
Goddesses unite
Unity…
Watching with the
Deer

Scorpio crescent moon
Grandfathr's birthday
A very special day!

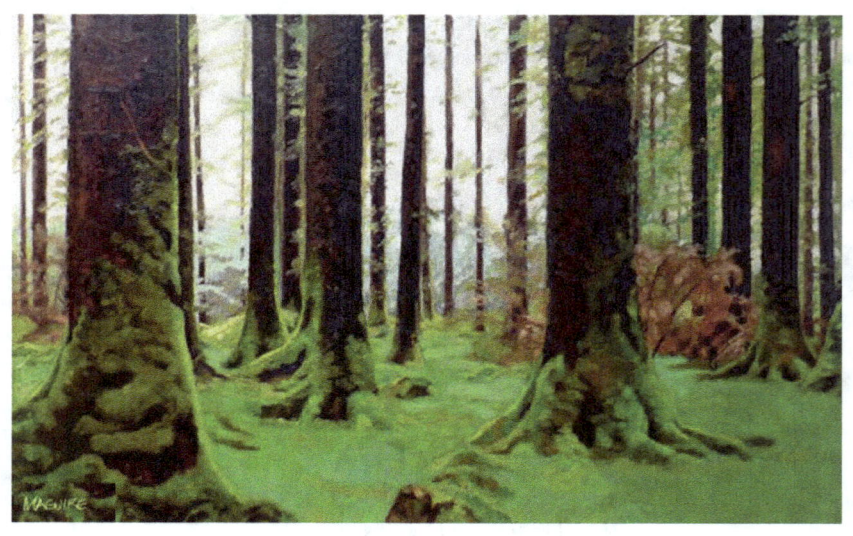

"Gougane Barra" oil   **Barrie Maguire**

THE MOSS

~ *Stacey Dexter*

I lay on my back across the warm settled moss, its cushion both prickly and soft. It covers an enormous boulder, stretched over it like a velvet linen cloak. The rocks' uneven, pointy edges nudge into my spine through the moss, into my sweatshirt, yet I am comfortable, soaking up the October sunshine, my chest filling and simmering with heat.

My head is even with the ground, my hair becoming damp from the morning's leftover dew. Black-brown leaves long past their prime are scrambled by a pushy wind. Crisp and dry, they are spread out over the rubble of the forest floor with mere inches between them — like scattered sunbathers at the beach on a hot August Saturday.

They remind me of my mistakes; too numerous, too far flung and out in the open, to collect. They are everywhere. But the moss; it effortlessly tumbles and tucks itself into each crack and crevice, segments stashed away, deep inside the rocks. I struggle to find a mysterious passage to hide my past, into some black tomb, that has no memory.

There is a fragrance in the breeze, the residue clean and unscathed. I'd like my life to be clean and unscathed, plump with newness and smooth edges. The ancient rocks, so much older than me, are more resilient, yet I feel older, not younger — crumbling and weak.

The invasive moss and the jagged rocks are comforting. Nothing here is spotless, perfect, or flawless. Me and my broken parts mix well with the orphaned leaves and the busted sticks, the uneven shades of dirt and the peeling branches. I want *this* life, peaceful and consistent. An inherent, deep rooted life. A neighborhood where I fit in.

The moss is silent. It multiplies with time, spreading its resilient, lush lichen upon the forest floor. It muffles the ground, stifling any sounds, almost tricking me into thinking that I am alone here. The thud from a falling pinecone, barely reaches my ears. It is quiet, lying on top of, and next to, the moss. My lips sealed with Chapstick, my breath weaves through my nose. No need to speak or explain. I am here in the stillness, in this moment, without fear.

Over time, the moss has been trodden upon by dogs and deer and meditative hikers; soaked and stung by bruising rainfall and left to suffocate under unforgiving layers of snow. Yet, it thrives and is revived with the seasons. It lives on in spite of...

I too, have been trodden upon—but by careless mutts and predatory mortals; abandoned in puddles of slick, salty tears, and suffocated under layers of human harshness. Yet, my breath returns and pushes through the cruelty, unraveling it like an old, wet woolen scarf, wrapped too tight around my head. I live on, in spite of...

But in the spring, the moss and I will welcome the new leaves; the stoic, steady boulders; the trill of robins and the April sun. I volunteer as tribute; decade after decade, stepping forward into this nurturing place, which provides me with a safeness I'm not used to. A gentle climate to exhale, feel consoled, and experience a revival—with my trusted and reliable Sister, the moss.

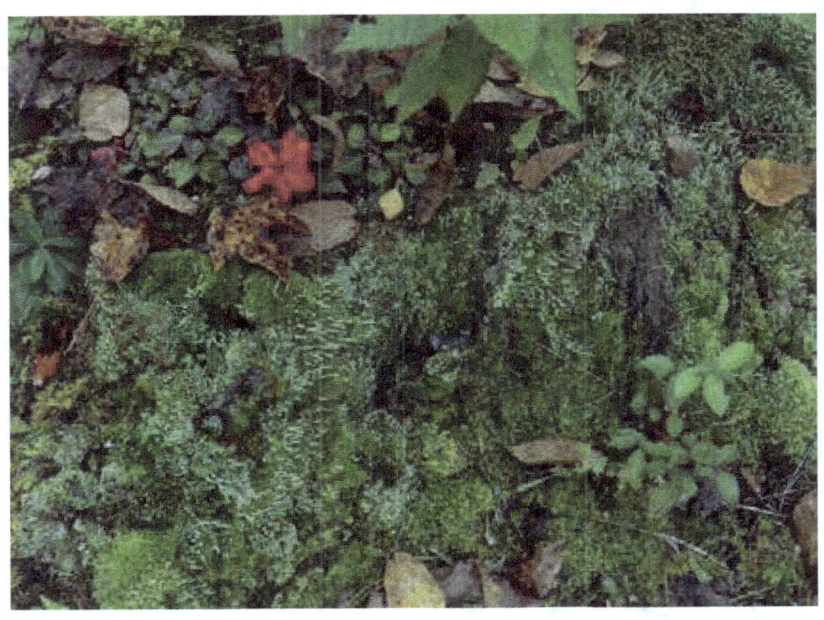

"Floor Moss" photo   ***Barrie Maguire***

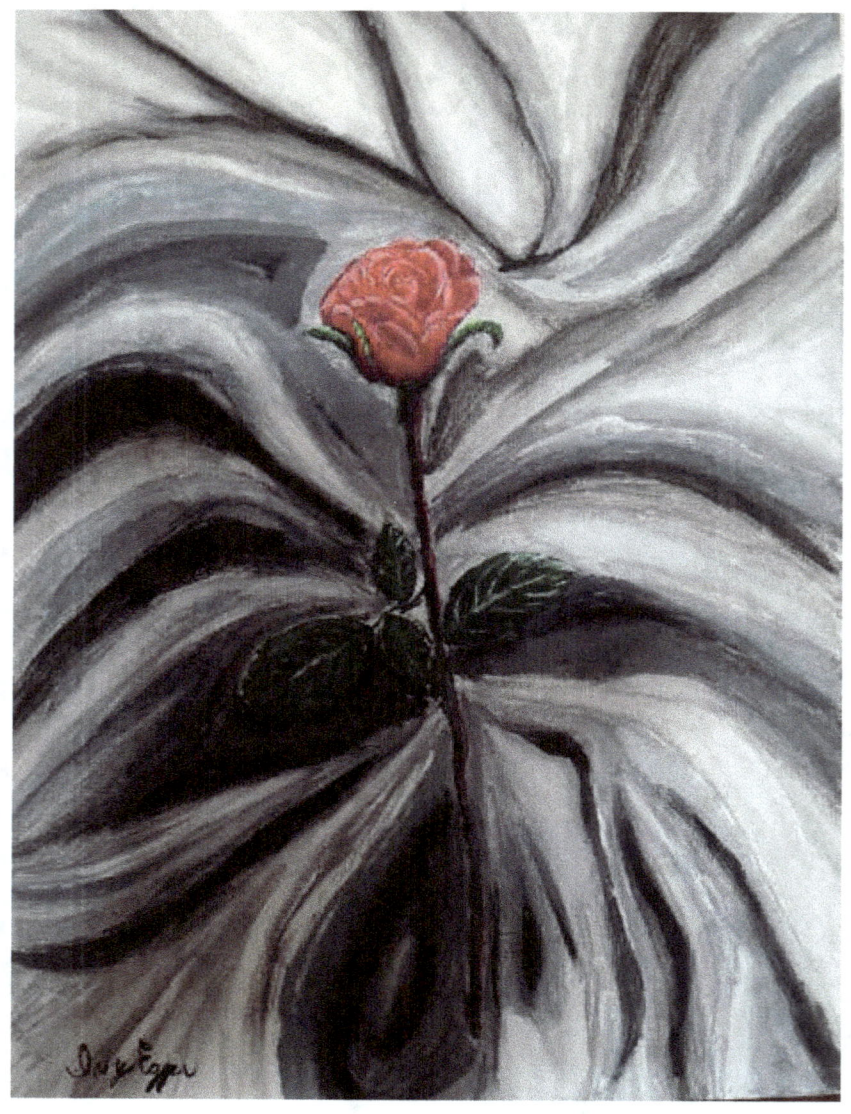

"Rose on the Grey" acrylic   ***Ivy Egger***

Our Trying Time

~*Jon Egger*

It was winter, with spring seeming distant.
We had a shot, and I was gone in an instant.
We were pregnant that fall, but to our dismay
It was not healthy, so I prayed.
I prayed that eventually our day would come.
Where we'd have our time to raise a daughter or son.
Well, that very winter was our best chance to conceive.
Yet somehow we missed, or so we believed.
But three weeks from then we eventually found that my wife's
flat belly would one day be round!
A higher power reminded us to always believe. He had a plan;
he meant for us to conceive.
That whole year would be filled with joy, and it came full circle
that autumn when we welcomed our boy.
Our trying time had brought us our forever of glee. For at its
conclusion, we'd have a family.

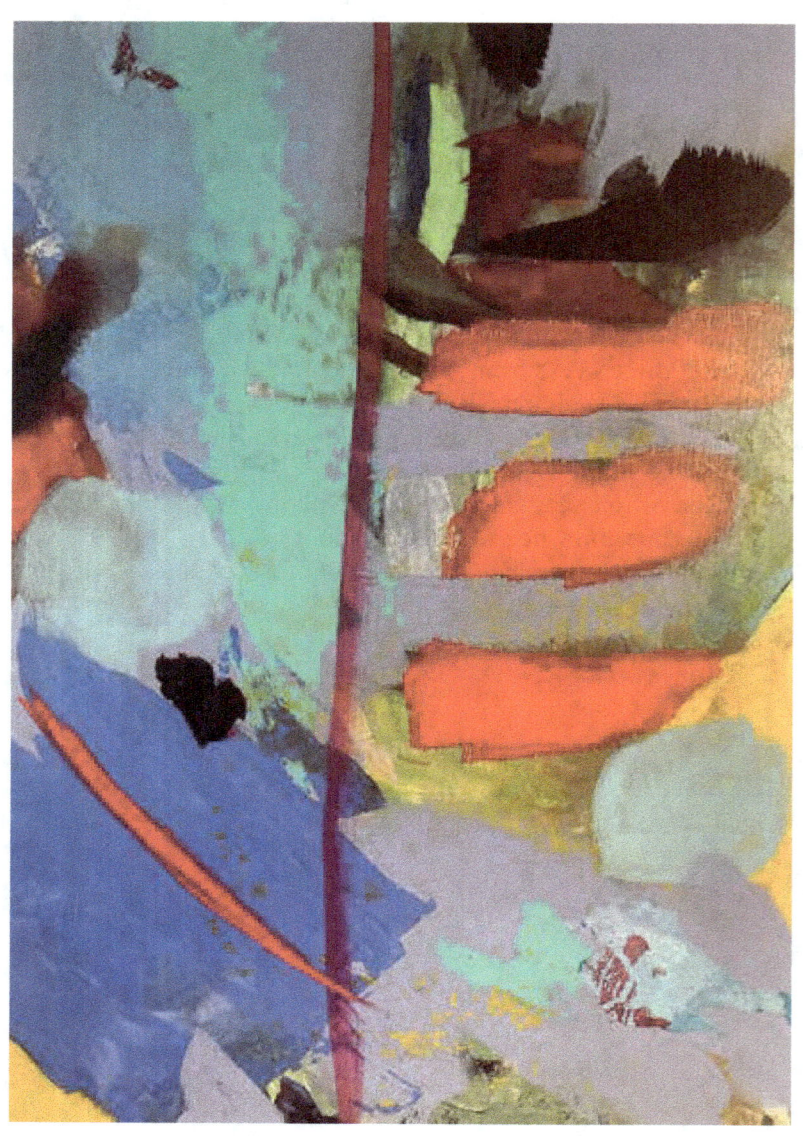

"Favorites" acrylic   **Suzanne Fellows**

My Favorite Things
~ *Andrew Fritz*

I hold these pure unsullied things close, like talismans.
The first two are Comprehension and its child Mastery. They make me greater, larger, better.
Then come the three Victory siblings: Possible, Certain, and Absolute. At first seeming to differ only in degree, experiencing each in turn is like tasting a new flavor or perceiving a new color. Possible Victory is a chance, a ray of hope rising over the dark horizon. Certain Victory is that hope fulfilled, all doubt banished. Absolute Victory is the removal of all future fears; the foe will never rise again. With its extinction comes Peace.
Smaller than these, but still treasured is True Justice, Justice enacted on the mortal plane and not hidden behind some afterlife veil. Offenders spend their days reaping the whirlwind, followed by a dinner consisting of crow with a side of humble pie and finished by just desserts, after which they lie in the bed they've made. Familiar metaphors, but when taken together, what a sweet bouquet!
The world can seem ugly, brutal, and unfair, but we have these gems amidst the slag and sewage. Hold them up to the light.
We need them.

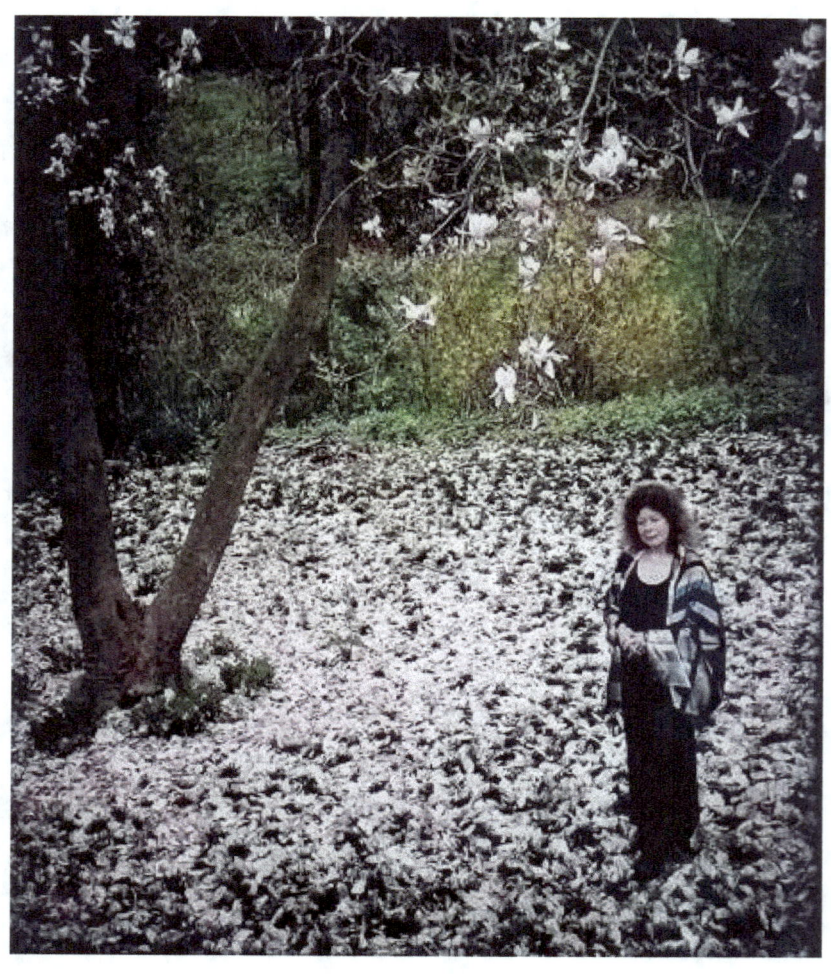

"My Mother's Picture" photo   *Jennifer Gittings-Dalton*

My Mother's Picture
~ *Jennifer Gittings-Dalton*

In the falling petals you stand, like a geisha of old Japan,
Wrapped in silk against the future you must have sensed arriving,
You look down, at the blossoms' epicenter on the ground,
Your small inward smile hinting at mystery: oh look—there is that!

There never was a time you didn't point where to see

Whether it was the flowers you arranged in a bowl,
The sketches of animals, always showing their tender bodies
Curled and vibrant, inexpressibly pure; the way you painted
The mothers and babies of the poor, Madonnas of the Andes,
Each woman real, looking up in hope and fear, each child held,
a Jesus, your images opened my heart to God in all Her particulars.

You sewed us our clothes, designed them, created beautiful homes
That let in light and wrapped us in color. You tried and sometimes failed
To keep us safe and healthy in countries all over the world.
You read to us, played with us, sang throughout the house.
You were young, you danced, you even liked the Beatles,
You gave us your youth, you overflowed.

There never was a time you didn't point the way

Here on the other end of that life, seeing it wrapped like a shell,
Like a flower that folds inward at day's end, I am breathless
At the beauty of your spirit. You faced illness and death with great
Courage, heedless of pain, cleaving close to life and to those who needed you.
Alone so much, you developed the soul of a monastic, communing
With birds, with the moon's face, a spray of leaves speaking for entire seasons.

As your body and mind weakened, you accepted and did not mourn,
And still you appreciated what little we did for you. I watched you
In secret pain, yearning for you to be freer, healthier, happier, little

knowing
You already had the secret, carrying your freedom within. You trusted
The God of the children, of animals, of sunsets and old women, to provide,
and He did. That God, you knew well: you were one of His innocents.

There never was a time you didn't show what to love

I must end this poem, which isn't the one I want to have written.
I, who never want to say goodbye to you, now find that I must.
I guess I will follow to where you stand, in your wisdom, under the pink tree,
And let you show me, with your slight, quiet smile, the rain of blossoms
Against your blouse, your hair, your hands, your life. Oh mother,
You were lent to me, and I am grateful. Nodding toward the earth, you
Take a step and are gone, like a dancer in a dream, in a mist,
And into your silence I reach but make no sound.

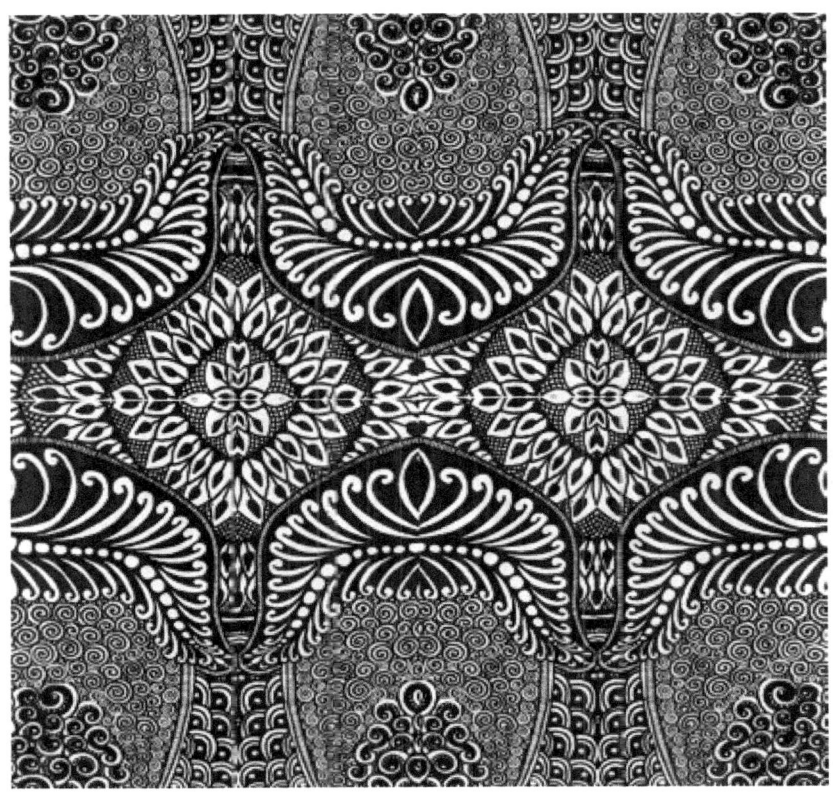

"Peacock Doodle" ink   **Beth Glick**

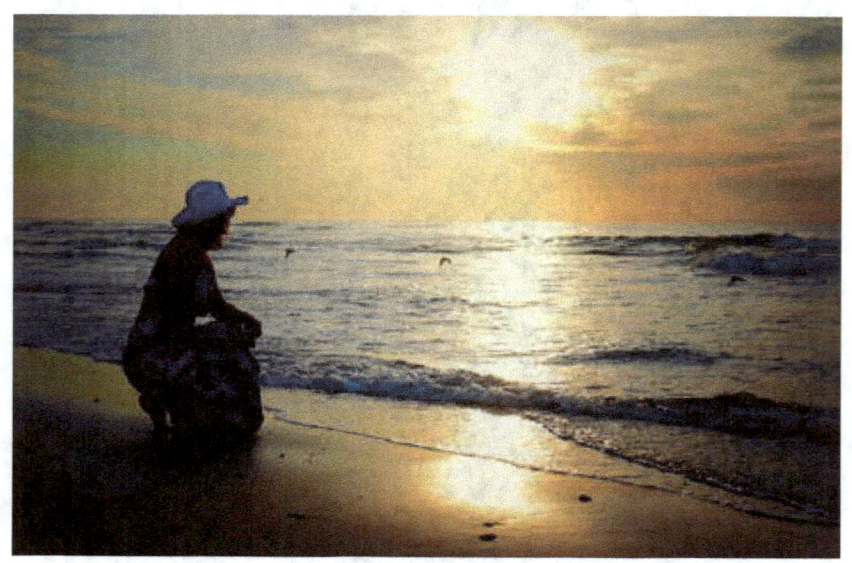

" The Hopes of Daybreak" photo   *Wendy Fox*

To Swim with Lilies

~Heather Goodman

In June, the water lilies sprout in the back bay where only kingfishers and great blue herons skulk. It's dark and mucky in the shallow cove, and still a bit like what you were afraid of as a child. There, Nymphaea odorata thrive, and by late August the lily pads have spread their audacious blooms out into the lake, snaking up through the watery depths as much as ten feet. Most of the time we admire them from afar, let them be.

But they are a miraculous thing, a blooming flower on the water's surface: white, perfect petals, gleaming yellow center. They are impossible and yet here.

And sometimes I can't help myself. I have to swim through them.

At their edge, I tread water, breathe in their heady perfume. I duck my head under the shroud of leaves, paddle downward once, then again. It's a creepy, haunting feeling, the trailing of their long stems, covered in a thin skim of algae, not so different than sweating skin. The lilies hold tight to the lake bottom, so there's tension as I brush against them, like a touch, with pressure and push.

I pull short strokes, try for smallness, careful not to kick so as not to rip the stems. I feel their eerie clutch, the snag of something pulling at the back of my heels, slippery tension about my wrist. It's the sensation of childhood nightmares: eels and snakes, menacing, thrilling.

Why do I crave this?

It's not the same just to swim at the lilies' edge—though I do that too. It's another thing entirely to swim into them, to be amongst them and their world.

Immersed in the lilies' lake, their stems arabesque-ing around me, luring me deeper—for these brief moments I'm a part of the inky, rich, deep, glacial lake; I'm trout and mink, snapping turtle and brown water snake. I'm of the lilies: dark and mystical, blooming and ephemeral.

And then I swim out of them, pause at their edge to watch the ripples glass out, the lilies still— and feel them drawing me back into a world where flowers bloom on water.

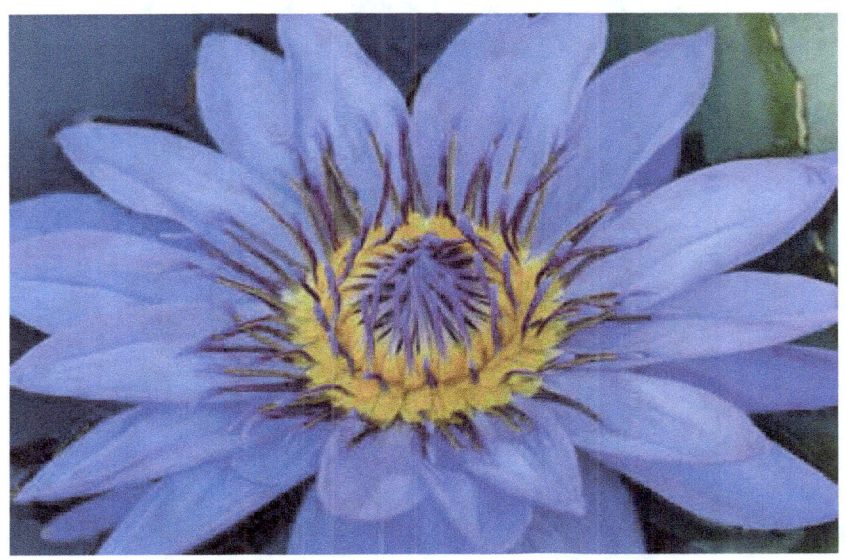

***"Petal Perfect"** photo* *Wendy Fox*

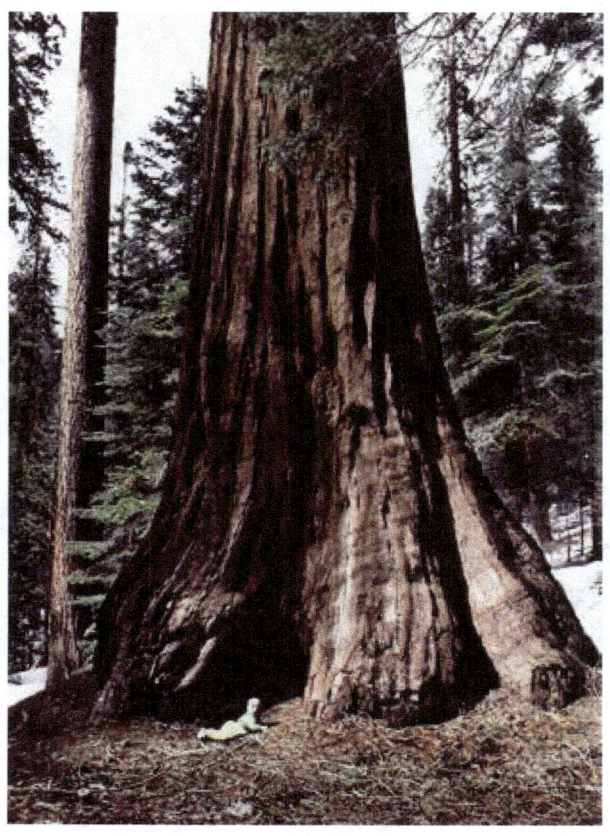

"White Oak" photo   *Walt Hug*

Many of us in the area know and have visited the Sacred Oak...a special yellow oak that has resided over generations of us, including native peoples. While hiking one day, I left a trail I normally take, and "bush-whacked" through some heavy growth in a dense section of woods that few people go. I soon discovered this immense white oak which called to me. I make a habit of visiting this old fellow and looked forward to feeling its ancient bark and spending time in its presence. Then one day not long ago, I was shocked and saddened to see "my tree" had fallen and its time had come, after hundreds of years. I offered my farewell and said a prayer. I was likely the only one who was aware of this magnificent tree...it was special only to me, and I mourned its passing. But of course it is now giving new life to the earth, animals, insects and plants that are transformed by it.
So go find your tree, and take in its beauty & spirit with its never-ending service of cleansing our air and Mother Earth.

The Transformation of an Old Friend

~ *Walt Hug (aka The Tree-Hugger)*

Find Your Special Tree
Spend Time in its Presence
Become Friends
And in Harmony
Whisper a Prayer
To this Gentle Giant
Touch its Venerable Bark
Take a Deep Breath
Give Thanks
Its Constant Cleansing the Planet
Exalt with the Spirit
Retrace the Path
To Its Lofty Home
Be its Guardian
And Mourn Its Passing
With Joy in the Transformation
Of New Life
Plant One in Remembrance
Born from the Offering
A Multitude of Renewal
Perpetual Gaia
The Wheel of Life

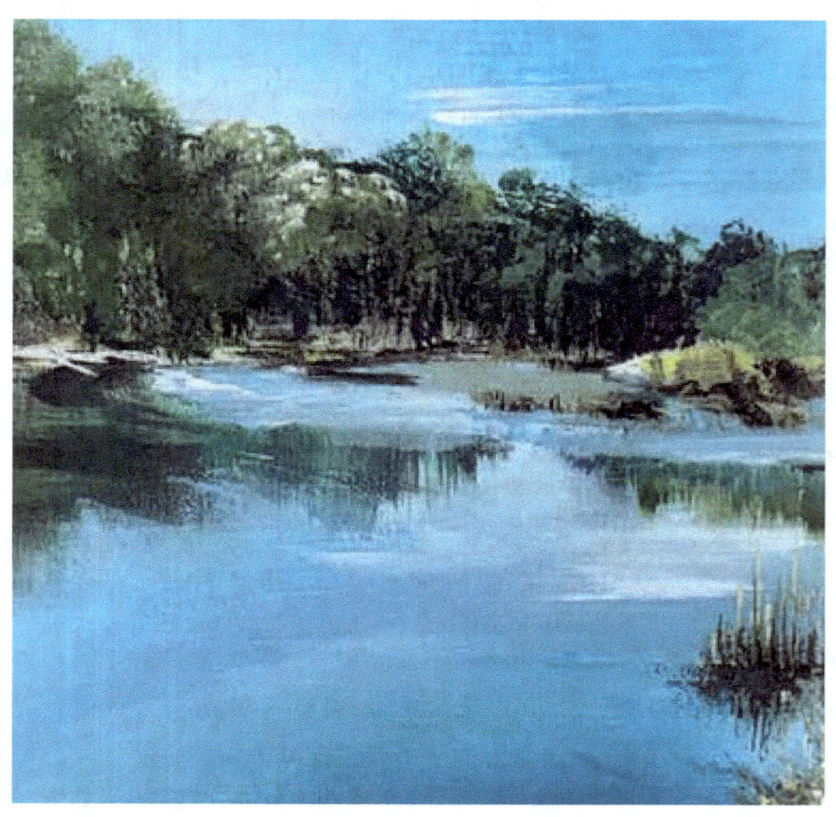

"Reflection of the Mind" oil *Joanne Moy*

Finding Happiness in a Different World
~ L.T. James

Dementia is a struggle
It's a thief! It robs you of your memory
Often your hearing and balance
It makes you feel afraid of how bad it will get
Will you even remember your wife's name
Who is with you every day
Watching the decline
And knowing it will get worse
But there is Happiness in this journey
Your loved one lives in the present
The past is gone or at the most
A dim memory
The future is but a dream
It could come true
Couldn't it?
It's today
And every day
Is a new day
Even though it seems to be the same day
Over and over again
Like the sun coming up each morning
And the moon sharing its light in the darkness

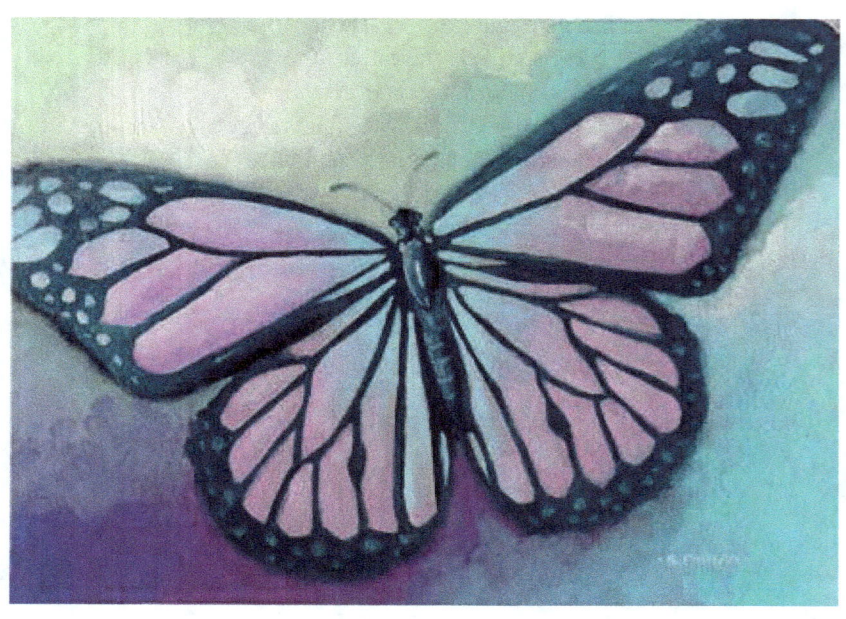

"Winds of Change" oil   *Steve Fabian*

Altar

~ *Kathryn Keegan*

The altar of my early years was marble,
hard and carved from solid ritual.
Now, the altar of my days
is a sacred space of small miracles,
soft as the powder of butterfly wings.

>Here lies a clay heart
>that only I know is pressed from
>thousands of grains of deep love
>
>a turtle shell
>filled with sweet desert sage
>gathered by a daughter's hand
>
>a chunk of beryl, rock
>green and chiseled holding secret places
>for momentary escape
>
>a shell from Sanibel
>plumed with found feathers
>still alert for the sound of sea
>
>a Chinese fortune cookie wisdom:
>the heart is wiser than the intellect,
>a blue jay wing
>
>skull bones bleached white
>from a lesson in mortality,
>a perfect nest, some crystal beads.

These gifts from the universe etch marks
deep as any grain in fine Italian marble.
This altar of cherished relics
is as precious as the earth I walk
where there is no place that is not sacred.

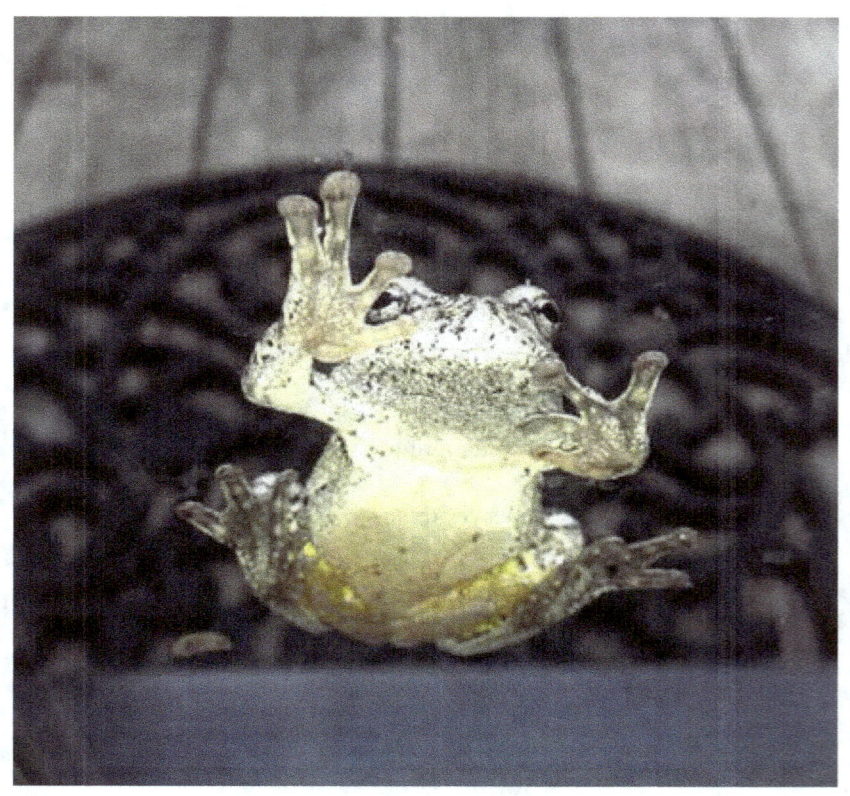

"Peeper on the Window"* photo**   ***Susan Biebuyck

Simple Marvels...

~ *Kathryn Kirk*

A blank sheet of paper,
A smoothly flowing pen...

Bright sun reflecting off fresh snow,
Nature's diamonds glistening...

Brisk winter air freezing nose hairs as the
Stars twinkle on black velvet...

Watching a bundled toddler
Discover the wonders of lights at night...

Shades of green and yellow in the distance...
Buds bursting at the seams...

Spring peepers chirping wildly on a
Warm vernal night...

Migratory visits of wood ducks
On a quiet pond...

Fireflies dancing in the
Darkness of summer...

Bold sunsets of vivid reds and golds
In hot hazy nightfall...

Bats diving for bugs over
The pond at eventide...

Multicolored leaves
Quivering in the autumn breeze...

Crisp air tainted with the
Scent of bonfires...

Stark branches quaking
In thin moonlight…

Cycles of life.
It's good to be alive.

A*PART

~ *Kathryn Kirk*

Apart, we're alone.
Join in to become a part
Of something bigger.

GRAND

~ *Kathryn Kirk*

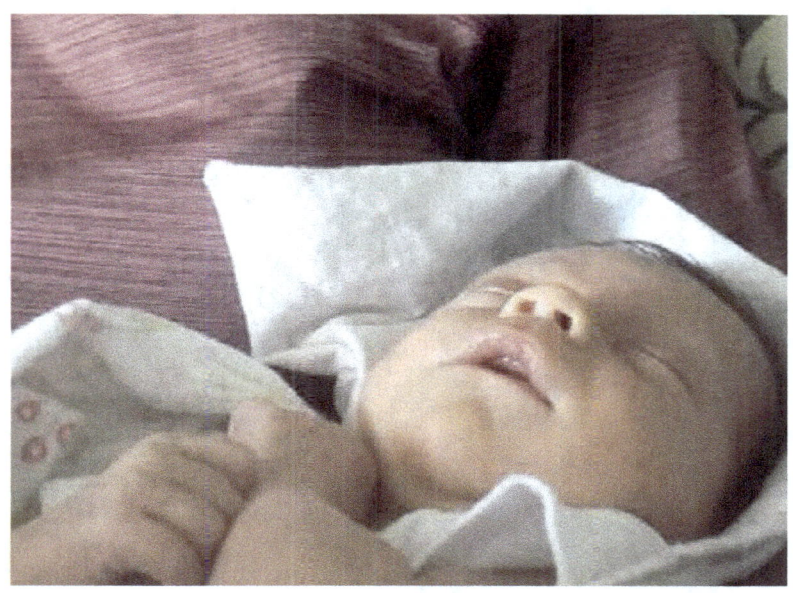

In my arms a child;
Through my blood, not of my blood
Joy and love abound

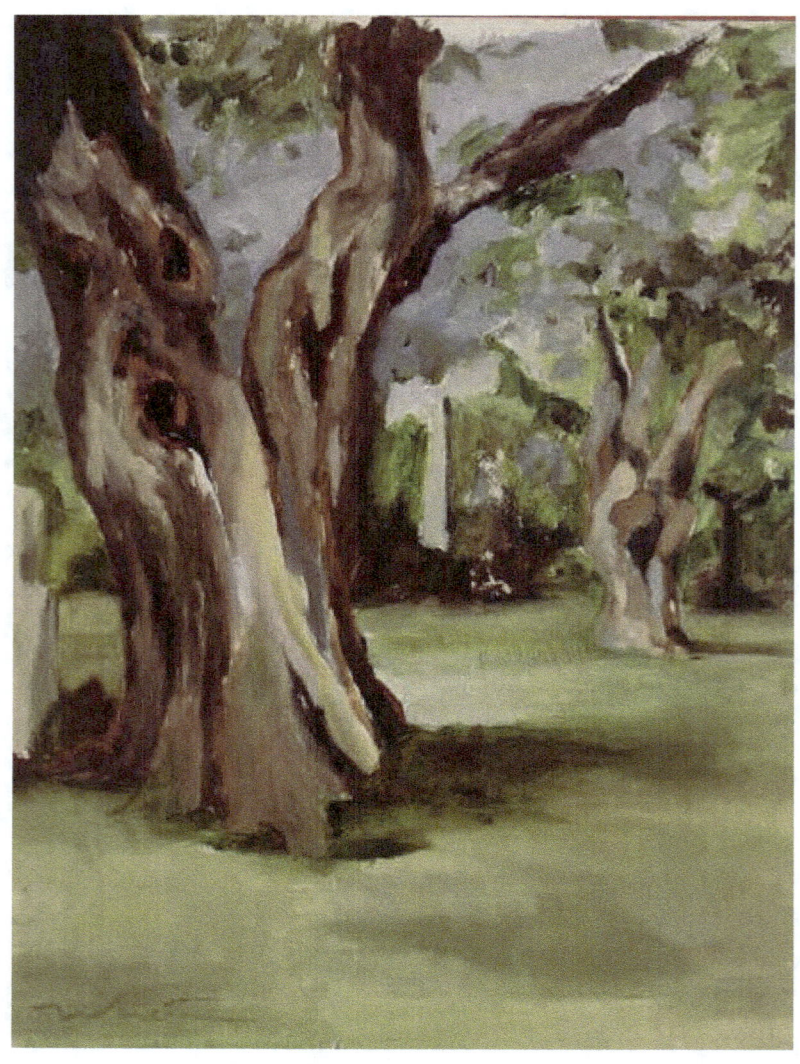

"Wisdom" oil   *Lauralynn White*

THE GREEN MAN
~ Marilyn Klimcho

The green man
Stirs like hope,
Like the great bones
Of a giant goaded
Into wakefulness.

Rattle the clay pots.
Bang the garden spade
Against the shed door.
Bite the sod
With tearing teeth.
Uproot winter!
Rake the scalp of lawn
Enough to make the grass
Stand up on end.

Be done with the
Flattening weight
Of parkas, head colds
And earmuffs.
Drag the spider-webbed
Lawn chair from the shed
Lay back and let a little
Chapped skin show.

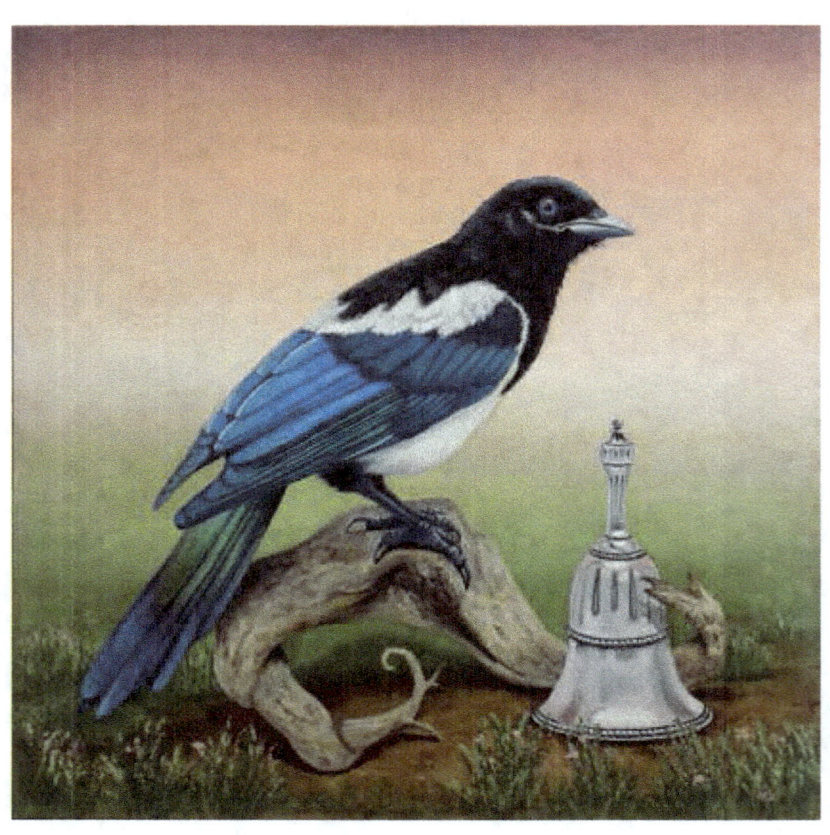

"Listening for Harmony" oil   *Kathryn E. Noska*

Things That Shine

~ *Virginia McNamara*

I've been living on Earth for seventy years now, and sometimes I wish I had journaled my life more often. But I if I'd done that, I might have lost sight of the exceptional experiences—the ones that quietly enthralled me and gave me hope, the ones that never lose their light. Those are the ones I store in my heart like jewels, bringing them out when I need them, letting them shine on me the way stars in a dark sky do, reminding me that there is something miraculous about being alive, even when the news media seems to say otherwise.

The common thread in those events is that they presented themselves while I was in a state of joy…or at least receptiveness. When I was present enough to take notice and appreciate the serendipity.

Many years ago, I was passing through an outdoor shopping center when I caught sight of a toddler who was facing a dilemma. She hesitated at the top of a four-step concrete staircase, unsure of herself. When she found the courage to try, I couldn't take my eyes away from the scene. I watched from a polite distance, but close enough to hear her father say 'good job' after each step down. After finishing the final step, she turned around to savor her accomplishment. Her smile made the rest of the world disappear.

When I want to deliberately attract something magical, I find a forest to explore and hope for something special to cross my path. But Nature has her own timetable and sometimes requires patience. There was that seemingly unremarkable hike, when a moose emerged from the woods at the exact moment that I told my husband: "I'm surprised we haven't seen much wildlife on this trip."

But there are also times when Nature finds me. I recall a particular morning meditation, the one where a cardinal showed up and sang continuously, quietly connecting me to a world with no worries. When I took the trash cans to the curb on a late summer evening,

Nature found me again—this time bombarding me with a chorus of crickets rollicking in the darkness.

Of all the treasures I've encountered in life, none shines brighter than Love—sometimes disguised as a simple kindness that appears without me having to ask. Ten years after it happened, I can still hear the voice of the stranger at the airport. Just as I'd set down the heavy suitcase to catch my breath, I'd seen his hand hovering over the luggage handle while gently asking "May I ?"

When I look back on past events, it's partly because I like to see where I've been. But I also know this: putting attention on things that open my heart creates a vibration that attracts even more favorite things.

Today, in the middle of January in eastern Pennsylvania, I'm appreciating the warmth of my kitchen when a flash of blue flies by my window and settles on a branch of a leafless tree. It's a male bluebird, looking in my direction, apparently waiting for me to notice him. I stare, motionless, expecting him to fly off at any second. But he stays. I rush to fetch binoculars, and now I can see his eyes and discern the rose and white down feathers, fluffed against the cold air. His appearance is a curious one, since eastern bluebirds normally migrate south for the winter and return in March. He waits until I hear what he came to tell me: that the world is full of wonders. And then he moves on.

Beauties Are Joys Forever

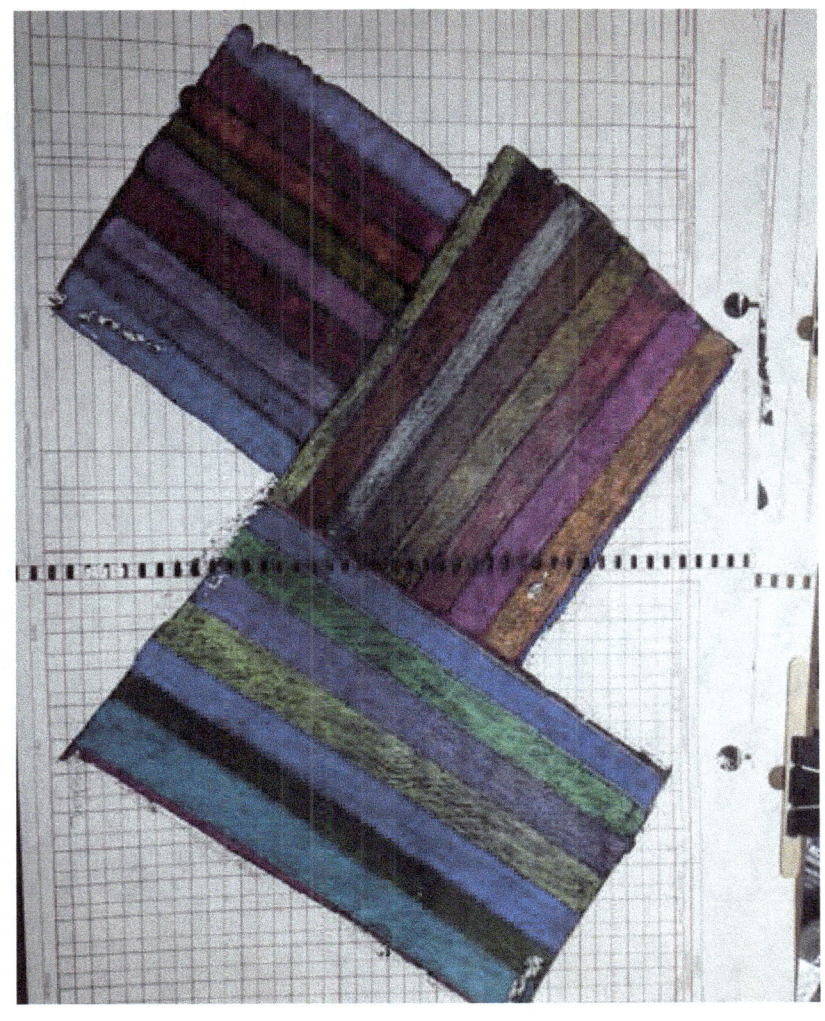

"Untitled" *drawing*   ***Ron Schira***

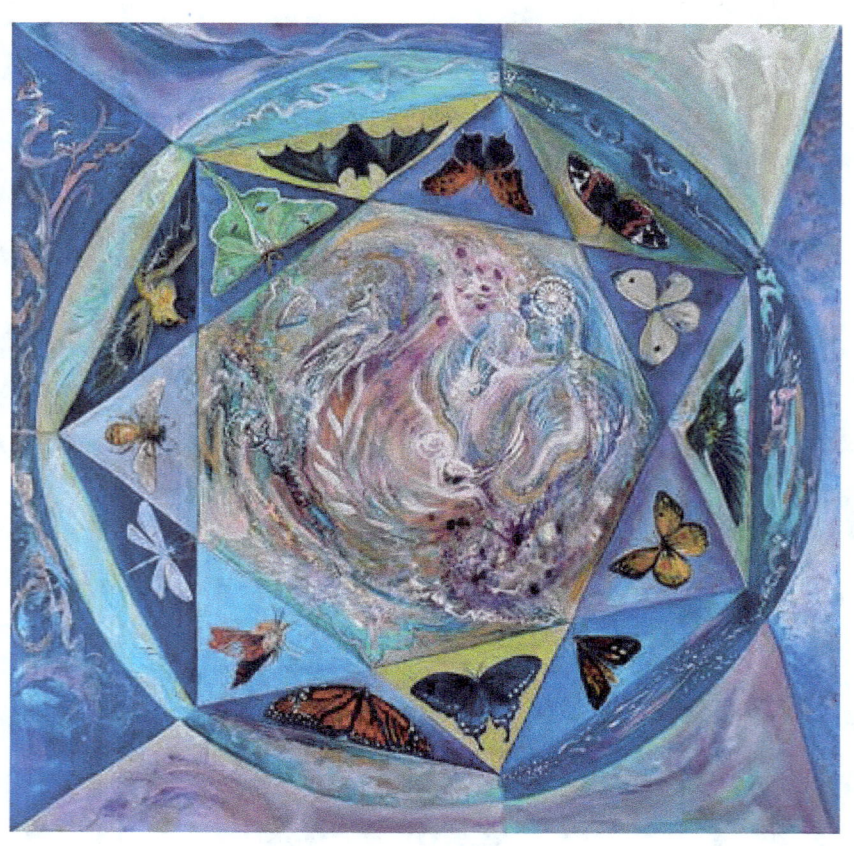

"The Pollinator Prayer" acrylic   *Victoria Lawrence*

DNA

~Lesley Huss Misko

The DNA of my youth
nestles among the bristles
of my brush,
Discovered after seeming centuries,
really only decades,
by touch,
as my hand searches
the back of a drawer,

A medium purple,
white swirled through.
A girl color.
An act of rebellion
from a girl whose mother
dressed her in browns and greens.

A long tail of plastic.
My thumb comes to a rest
on the place intended
so I could tease my hair.
Hair wasn't the only thing
I teased.

Eddie and Freddy,
Peter and Joe.
Ken and Lester,
Joe again – always –
And David – a BIG mistake.
Teasing hair was
a means to an end.

My hand hovers mid-air,
over the front of the drawer,
But I recoil at disturbing
the DNA of my youth,
And I return the golden strands

to the darkness at the back,
Perhaps to be discovered
When I am gone.

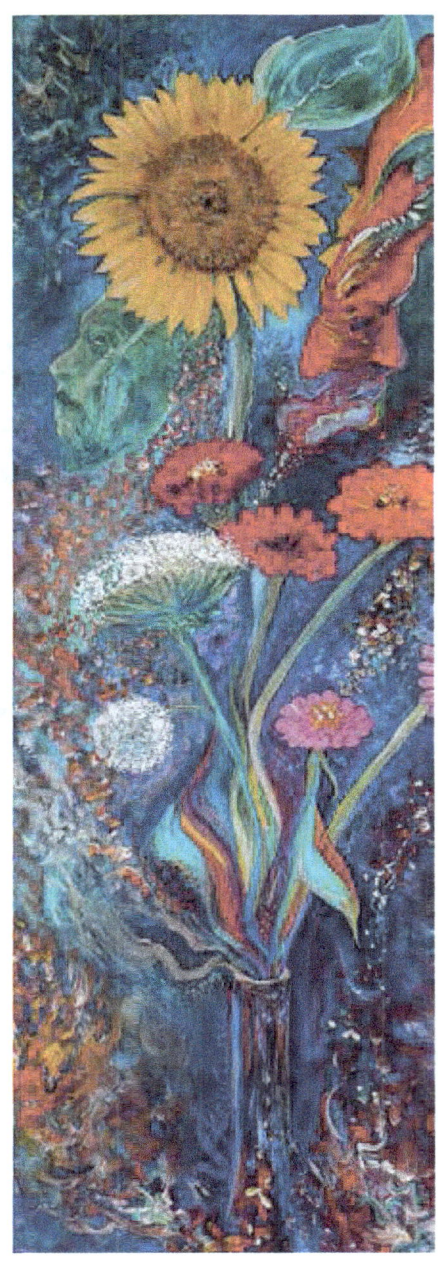

"Pomona and Vertumnus" acrylic   *Victoria Lawrence*

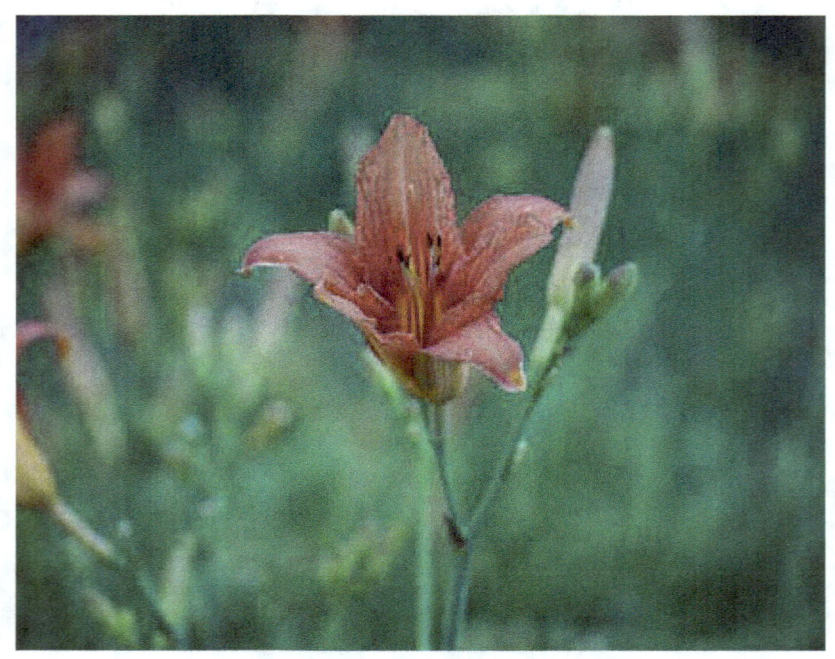

***"Blooms Stand Tall"** photo*   *Lisa Mitchell*

BLOOMS STAND TALL
~ *Lisa Mitchell*

Dark clouds loom,
Overhead a menace,
Warning of the impending storm.

A strong wind blows,
Vengeful and cruel,
Destroying all in its path.

Yet new life grows,
A promise of tomorrow,
Breaking through the damp earth.

Vivid green shoots up,
Small but mighty,
Pushing through strangling vines.

Rain drops heavy,
Bitter and cold,
Pounding on delicate blossoms.

A light shines,
Bright and warm,
Breaking through the dark clouds.

Blooms stand tall,
Bold and colorful,
Reaching for the light.

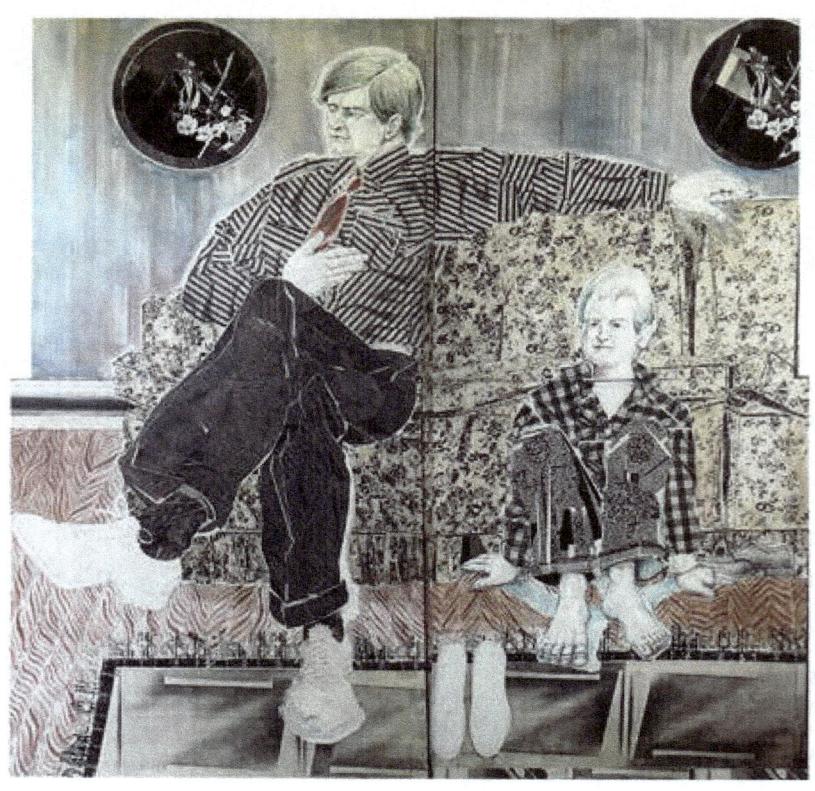

"Tony & Joe" mixed media   *Jim Meehan*

HAZEL

~ *Clemson Page*

Rain squalls splattered against the windows of Evelyn Walker's fourth-grade classroom at Penn Valley School in the Philadelphia suburbs on a dark October afternoon in 1954. "Forerunners" Miss Walker called them, using a storm threat as a teaching opportunity. Hurricane Hazel was moving up the coast from her landfall between the Carolinas; these "forerunners" were a promise of heavier weather to come.

We fourth-graders found it hugely exciting. It was Friday, October 15th; school was probably going to dismiss us early – a prospect which gave things a festive, holiday air. A little rain didn't seem all that scary. Even (as it was) a lot of rain.

The hurricane wind didn't start in earnest until after I'd gotten home. How I got home I don't remember. Behind battened-down doors and windows, in the early post-equinoctial darkness, Hazel seemed to peer in at us through obsidian black panes, with massive meteorological indifference – as if she had us trapped and would deal with us at her convenience. From where we sheltered, it still didn't seem like much out there. Mom gathered candles, flashlights, batteries, and a single kerosene lantern. She tuned the big console radio in the living room to follow the storm broadcasts, and we waited. Dad came home from his office. It wasn't long before the power went out. Darkness ensued. The radio storm bulletins ceased.

My parents, two brothers and I lived as tenants in the roomy five-bedroom residential apartment adjacent to and above a four-bay garage that housed our family car, the chauffeur's car, and two other cars owned by the landlords of the J.D. Winsor estate – including a big, long shiny black Buick town car in which Thomas Murray, dressed in formal livery, chauffeured the lord and lady of the manor about their ceremonial worldly affairs. Murray spent his days in a comfortable ground-floor apartment adjoining the garage structure, within easy reach of the two-way telephone which connected the garage and the "Big House" a quarter-mile across the apple orchard, by which a summons for transport could come, sometimes with little or no prior warning. Among other things, buried beneath that garage was a tank containing (when full) 300 gallons of gasoline, connected to a hand-cranked pump and a filler hose. The Winsors purchased their coal, oil, and gasoline in bulk.

The cozy atmosphere in the dark, fire-lit house was heady stuff for a nine-year-old boy. The big coal-fired furnace in the basement kept the steam radiators hissing and banging, filling the house with the comforting aroma of hot iron. We may have been in the dark, but we were not chilly.

My father had nourished his sons' imaginations with a steady diet of bedtime stories – <u>The Voyages of Doctor Dolittle</u>, <u>The Swiss Family Robinson</u>, and similar fare. It didn't take a big imagination to transport us to a place much more fraught with adventure than 101 Cherry Lane, Ardmore. I loved it.

Sometime in the night, there came a sharp CRACK! from out in the storm. No one investigated at the time.

If the wind howled, I slept soundly through it.

Saturday dawned bright and sunny. The only nearby signs of the hurricane were downed branches, a continued absence of electric power, and – source of the loud noise from the night before – one-half of a giant double-trunk Osage orange tree which had fallen across the driveway, blocking passage to and from the garage complex via the upper driveway. Providentially, the windfall blocked only the tradesmen's driveway; except for a few bundles of branches and brush, the main drive out the lower gate remained clear and passable.

After a cold snack, and still without power for cooking, we piled into the family station wagon to go survey the effects of the storm beyond our immediate bailiwick -- and, not incidentally, to find some hot food.

The landscape beyond our domain was a tangle of downed trees and power lines. Heavy equipment and crews labored to clear the lanes and roadways, so only a few detours were necessary. First we went to visit our family friends the Reads, who lived several miles away in a big converted two-story chicken coop surrounded by mature hardwood trees on a local gentleman's farm. Howard Read greeted us and showed us to an upstairs closet where a sizable portion of the trunk of a large tree protruded through the ceiling. The vision has stayed with me over the years as an image of disaster and destruction – haunting me in the recesses of my imagination even after I grasped the concepts of casualty insurance and damage restoration some years later.

After our view of Hazel's depredations in the Read house, reality struck with redoubled hunger pangs and cravings for hot food. We set out in caravan with the Reads in search of a meal. We fetched up in a booth at Jim & Bill's Mari-Nay Diner near the Rosemont commuter rail station on the Main Line. Hot soup, saltines, a couple of hamburgers, and a chocolate milkshake laid Starvation to rest in my system for the time being. We finished our survey of the storm damage and returned home.

The Osage orange tree wreckage had been cleared from the driveway, but still remained beside the drive, where for weeks the tree's sturdy carcass served my brothers and me and our friends as a fortress, spaceship, battle station, hiding place, and refuge from adults. I'll never forget the pungent, lemony smell of freshly - felled Osage timber.

Later in the day, it appeared from the Philadelphia Electric service trucks gathering in the vicinity that power was about to be restored. This seemed a shame to me, so captivating had it been to shelter by firelight from the darkness the night before. I was not ready for a return to incandescent lighting, radio communications, television (primitive as it was in those days). Something had to be done – quickly.

I knew the fuse box was at the foot of the cellar stairs. I knew a little about how electricity worked. It was a mere matter of minutes to go down the stairs, open the fuse box, unscrew the fuses, and go nonchalantly about my business as our world plunged back into autumnal darkness. Our folks lit candles and kindled the hearth, and we returned to the storybook world of the previous night.

I had forgotten about the telephone. It rang. Dad answered. He didn't say much. He hung up, took a flashlight, and descended the cellar stairs. It was a mere matter of minutes before once again incandescent lighting, radio communications, television (primitive as it was in those days) returned to my world.

There followed no formal inquisition as to who had monkeyed with the fuses. The question did arise, however.

Dad gave me a grin and a wink.

"I bet Hazel did it," he said.

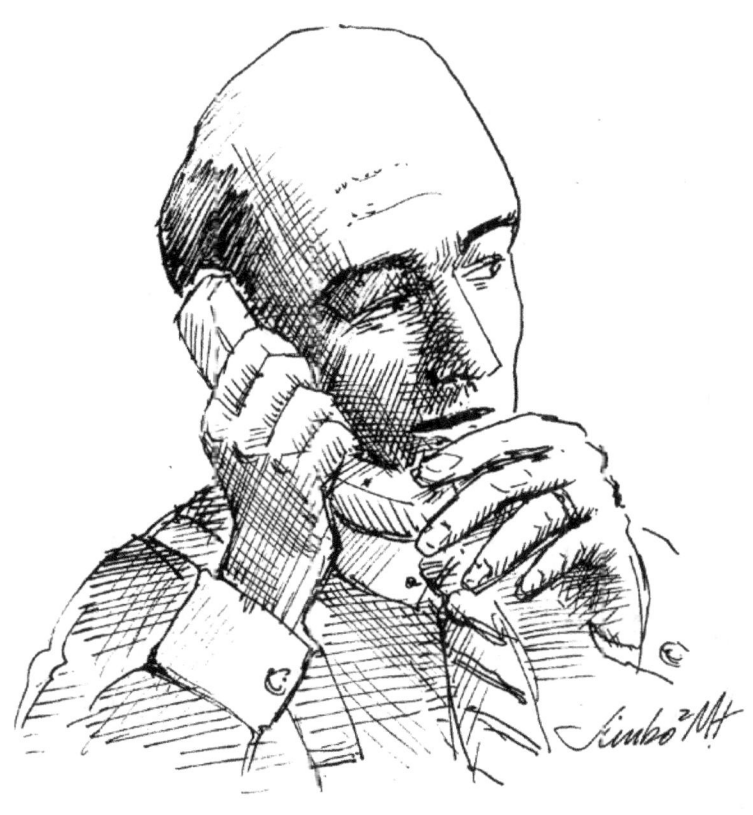

"Just a Guy on the Phone" ink   *Jim Meehan*

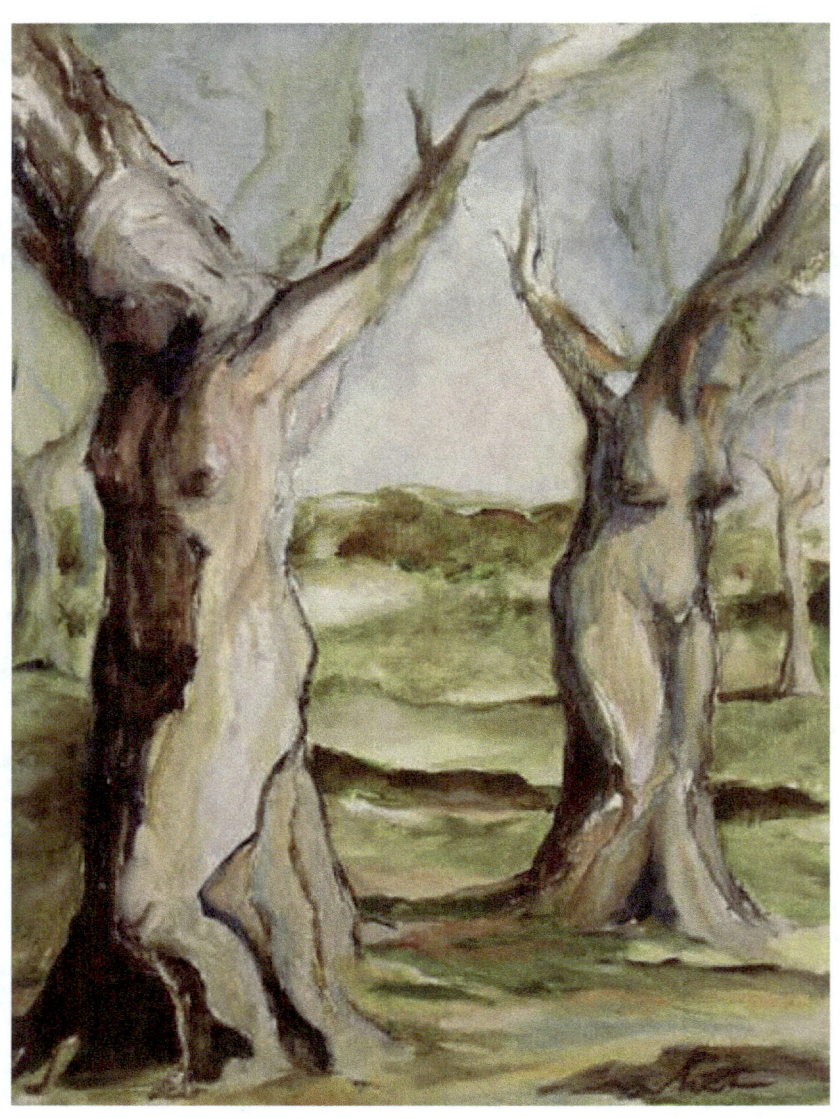

"Languor" oil   **Lauralynn White**

Perpetuate...
~ *Philip Repko*

I was one of many leaves that sprouted
from the Family Tree, and shouted,
"There! No, there!"
In games of Hide and Seek without a care -
Except for running noses, bogeymen, and bears...
Except for stubbing toes's, games of do's and dares -
Nine little indians were we,
our cowboy neighbors saddled strong Schwinn steeds,
Or flex'ble Flyer mounts in January's freeze
we held them off until they called the cavalry,
or Sergeant mothers sounded full retreat,
and battles ceased until we scurried home to eat.

Left to our own devices, we
became our own best friends, you see -
Sharing lies, and cries, and sighs
and racing under summer skies
to all points West, the general store
for nickel Cokes and ten-cent Hershey bars;
Or else we'd head to haunted 'ghost town' camps,
In cut-off shorts, the little children village tramps-
Made friends with old canoes who wanted company
so waded shaded rivers amid symphony
of cricket strings, and wood-peckered percussion,
accompanied by muddy waters rushing,
Our thoughts uncluttered by a troubled world
Forbade to touch us smiling boys and girls,
who sported scrapes and scabs on sun-kissed skin
Made darker still by dirt and dust found in
Abandoned barns made country playground pens
for games of dodge ball, kick the can, and then...

Quite mobile yellow prisons took us one by one away
to separate cells to live together,
"Hey!"
And somehow, strangely, somehow, in a day
We rode together to our own small way.

And then that family tree grew much in size
With strong new leaves and limbs, but those old ties
grew weaker at the root, stretched out to follow
the branches splayed apart; its trunk grown hollow,
Decayed at core, deprived of family blood,
which yesterday would sate and sometimes flood,
but now oft trickles, slow, the breach between
forever widens, though it creeps unseen.

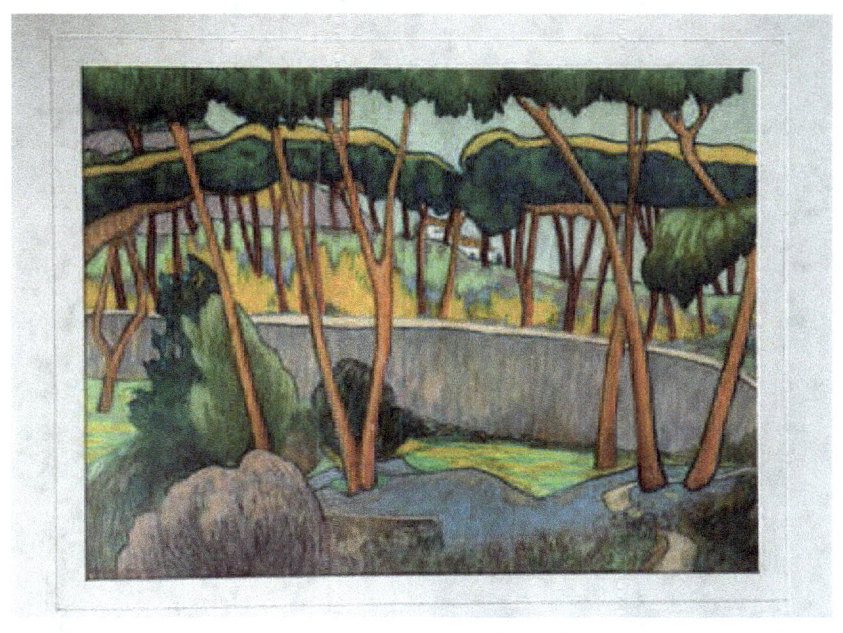

"A Walk in the Woods" pastel   *Nancy Lang Boyer*

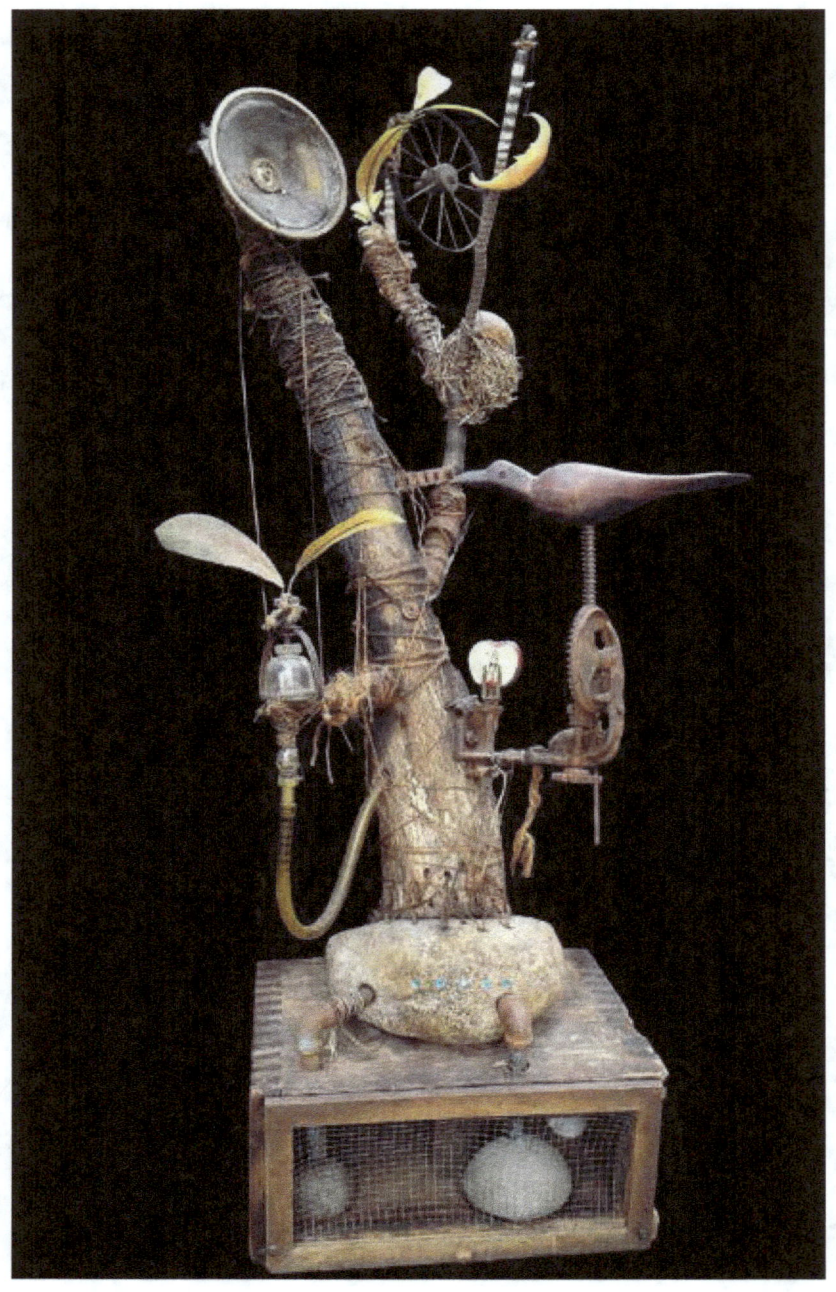

"Music of the Stones" assemblage — **Bob Hakun**

A Branch of Me
~*Philip Repko*

Young boy in me will make me ape
Cro-Magnon Man with lumbering gait,
Low furrowed bow, large hairy fist -
A walking stick, the catalyst

A cool, shale day; fine whispering rain
When boy and I went out to play
Aware of Autumn's whistling tune
and mist on chilly skin.

We ran, yelled, sang; discovered stuff -
small pine cones, mud prints, hurrying squirrels.
We walked across a rotting log
-and teetered-
Then we fell.

He saw it first, a fallen limb;
Not quite a club, but not so thin
To be a little twig. It was
A spear, a weapon, everything.

Before we skipped, but now we trod.
We braved a treacherous ebony bog.
(A water puddle really, clear.
Sharp Truth's submerged in what we feel.)

A branch of spruce; perhaps of elm
Familiar in my knotty palm.
We flail at anything that's near,
And echoes crack of early years.
We feel out of - and in - control.
He looks at me.
I know.

A branch of me; a branch for him;
Now we are mortal enemies.

He turns to show me deadly eyes.
He circles, javelin held high...

A nervous laugh, uneasy smile -
We walk an eerie, weary mile.
He does not call me Daddy 'til we're home.
He drops the stick, but finds a femur bone.

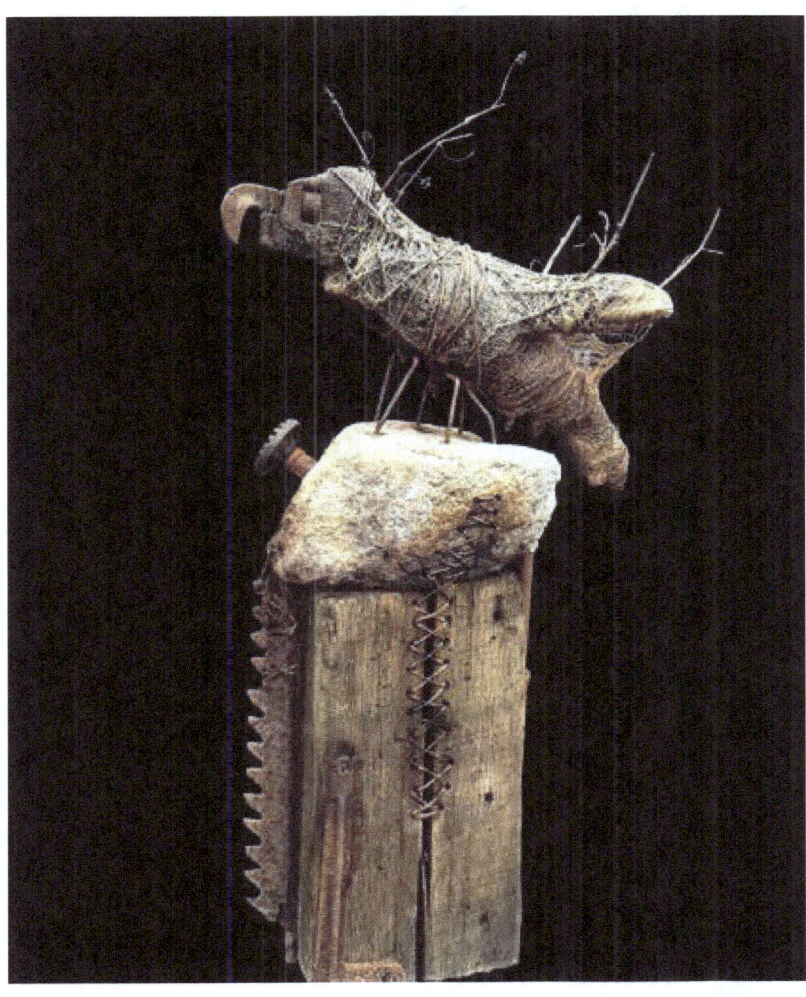

"Twig Bird" assemblage — ***Bob Hakun***

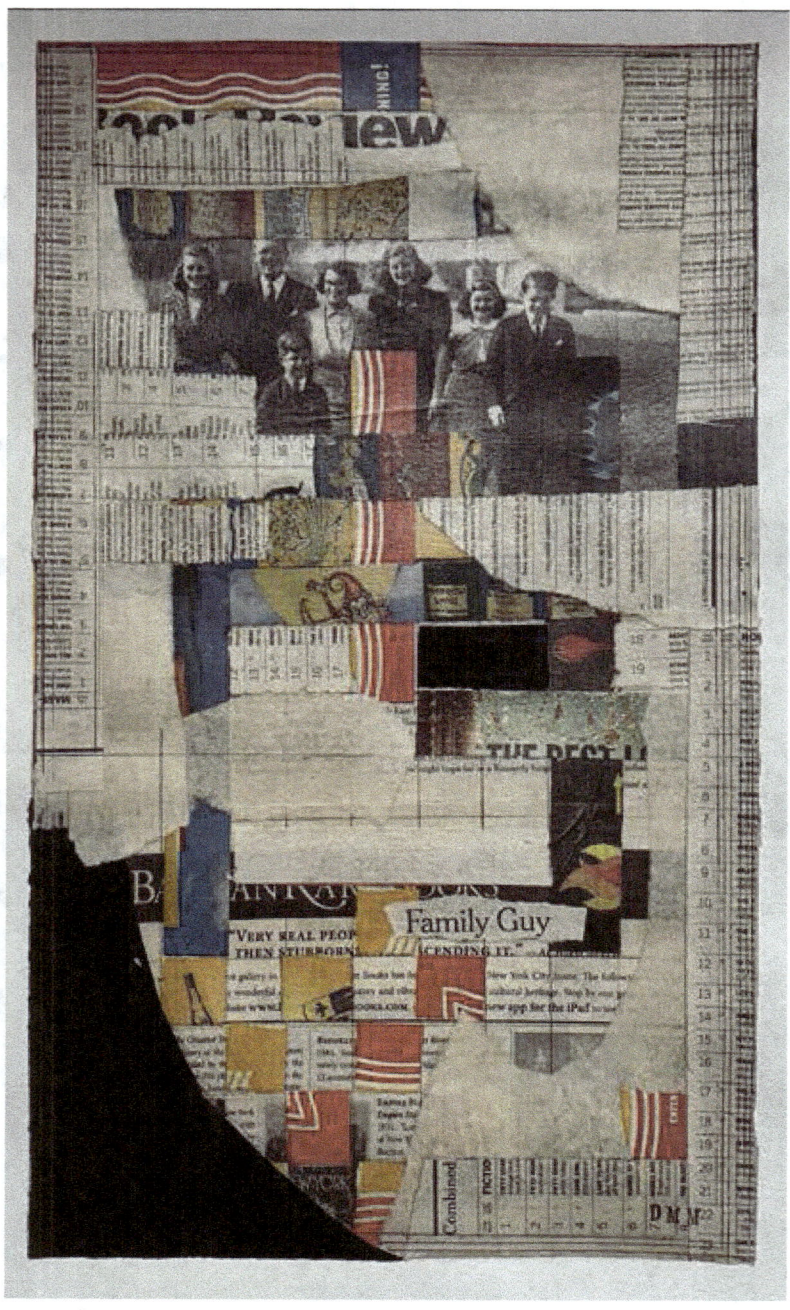

"Family Guy" collage   Deborah Maguire Meehan

REUNION

~ *Philip Repko*

It is a pulsing pageant of cliches
A made-in. All-American parade
Of home-baked apple pie and backyard games.
"It's such a shame, Aunt Dotty passed away."
"I say it's such a shame," then louder still,
But Uncle Bill, a great third cousin, will
Not hear or understand. He's far away
Attending splendid picnics long since paste,
Though he sees diamonds, baseball mitts, and bats
The rough-edged belfry, jostling all that's past.

With coats of arms and heraldry they come
In caravans from all across one place,
To drink the hours dry before they're done,
With milk and honey smiles on each face.
They find the silver linings in a sun
That reads the wrinkles time has kindly placed
As we've grown up, or old, or slipped away.

They reconnect in person – face-to-face.
Renewing ties that tremble taut and sere,
They memorize the joy the years have traced,
Before the march outstrips the now and here.
Because the march of years is not all kind.
All families suffer tragedies and loss.
But once each year, at least, they take the time
To honor all the love and cry the cost.

Reviving family folklore flows its course,
Upheaving stories buried musty deep
In cedar chests immortalized by scents
From 1963? We'll give or take
A decade's worth of smoldering each June.
The tales fill in the blanks – and resonate.
As aromatic whispers share the tune.

My Favorite Things

Now Uncle Matt plays partner here with me
In horseshoe tournaments where no one wins,
Because the score we keep is musical
And passages of time stay razor thin.
The folding chairs, aluminum, and light
Serve purposes more metaphorical
Than any softness or support in sight
The comfort offered more apocryphal.
But sights bring only joy and weightless mirth.
The toddlers, these living dust balls run
Through canopies of bright Bermuda shorts
And watercolor blouses gossamer –
To beat the late July relentless heat.
The rivulets of sweat find liver spots
On necks and hands that once touched history.
These souls have more prevailed than just endured,
Reminding younger ones to stay their course.

There's food and beer and favorite recipes
Passed down through generations far and wide –
But reconvened each summer for a time,
Ingredients are shared, and always prized.
Great Uncle Buddy brings a casserole.
Another cousin fancies apple cake.
The younger ones blow bubbles near the lake,
While teens roll eyes, embarrassed by old souls
Who seem to know the wrong approach to take?

Reluctantly the shades of dusk arrive.
The signal sounds that family fun must end,
Though stories linger long and soar aloft,
Connections staying hardy, firm, but soft.
Like tails of paper kites, the stories soar
Upon the winds in strange, familiar time.
Oft buffeted by storms of awesome force,
But also, much resilient in the line
Of tattered years linked tightly one to one –
In shadowed pantomime they shade the day
As families now head homeward on their ways.

And like those kites, just subject to the breeze.
Some folks will float and some stay anchored tight,
While others still will feel the tethers sneeze -
Exaggerating distances through flight.
It's harder still to find the list of names
That constitute the patchwork family tree –
Some strings grow frayed and harshly snap away
So disconnected faces stay unseen.

Now it's been twenty years since last they came,
And yes, the list is long of those who've left,
To venture to the greatest picnic yet,
Where all may be united once again.
But, oh those sights and smells still register,
As clear and crisp and vibrant as before.
We have a way to miss the ones we've seen,
And feel the pang of loss forevermore.

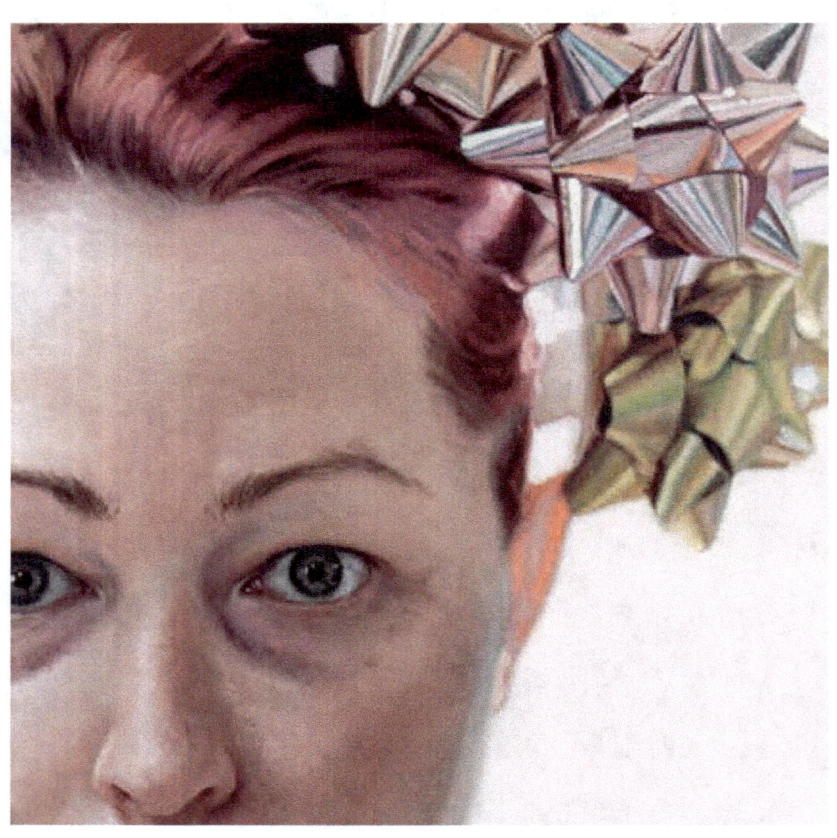

"Spotlight" oil   *Hilary Swingle*

My Journal

~ *Theresa Rodriguez*

Within my world there is a sacred place,
Where I can hide and then reveal my heart;
Where thoughts and feelings go, and become art;
It is a sanctuary, hallowed space.
Creating something new and touched with grace,
I put my mind to pen, and then impart
My soul's outpourings through my mind, to start,
Then show my whole raw self with open face.

And when complete, I then perfect my words,
And get them ready for the world to see;
I take them from these pages, then display
Them out for those who read, and hear. This girds
Me up for naked vulnerability.
Indeed, I offer all I am this way.

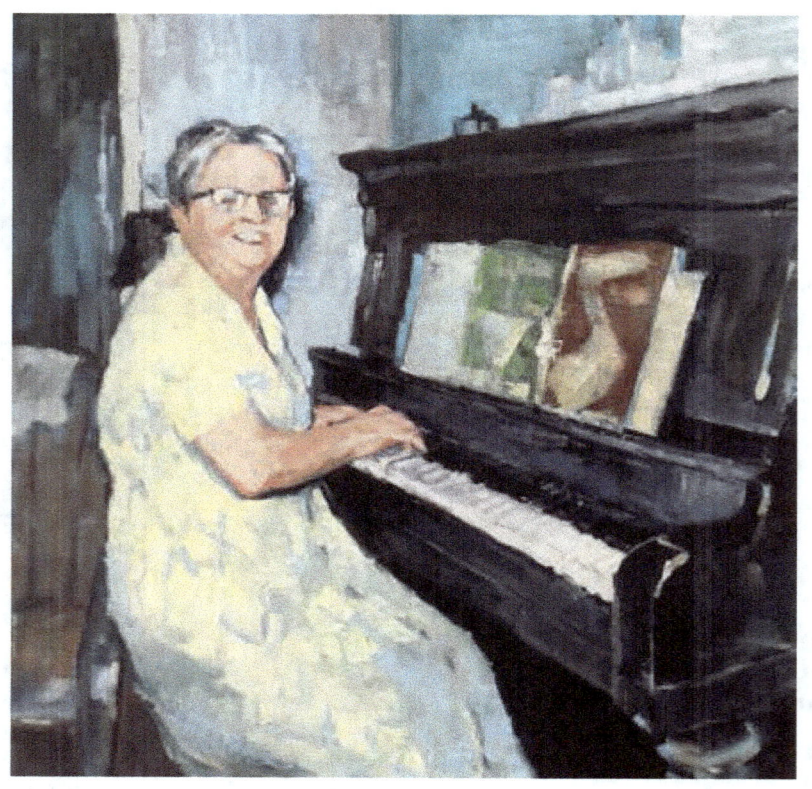

"Sing-Along" oil   *Marianne Buschini*

STEINWAY PANTOUM

~ *Theresa Rodriguez*

How can I love an object like I do?
It's almost like I have a lover's heart
and I'm in love. But do not misconstrue,
somehow it works in sync, in counterpart!

It's almost like I have a lover's heart:
I wish to make love as I touch the keys
somehow; it works-- in sync, in counterpart,
and like two lovers, who will give and please.

I wish to make love; as I touch the keys
I play, and somehow it responds in kind;
and like two lovers, who will give and please--
its tone the sweetest gifting to my mind.

I play, and somehow it responds in kind
and offers up a most unearthly sound:
its tone the sweetest gifting. To my mind,
responsiveness in action rarely found,

and offers up a most unearthly sound.
The lover and beloved combined as one;
responsiveness in action rarely found,
to touch perfection, not to be outdone.

The lover and beloved, combined as one,
and I'm in love! But do not misconstrue.
To touch perfection, not to be outdone
how can I love an object like I do?

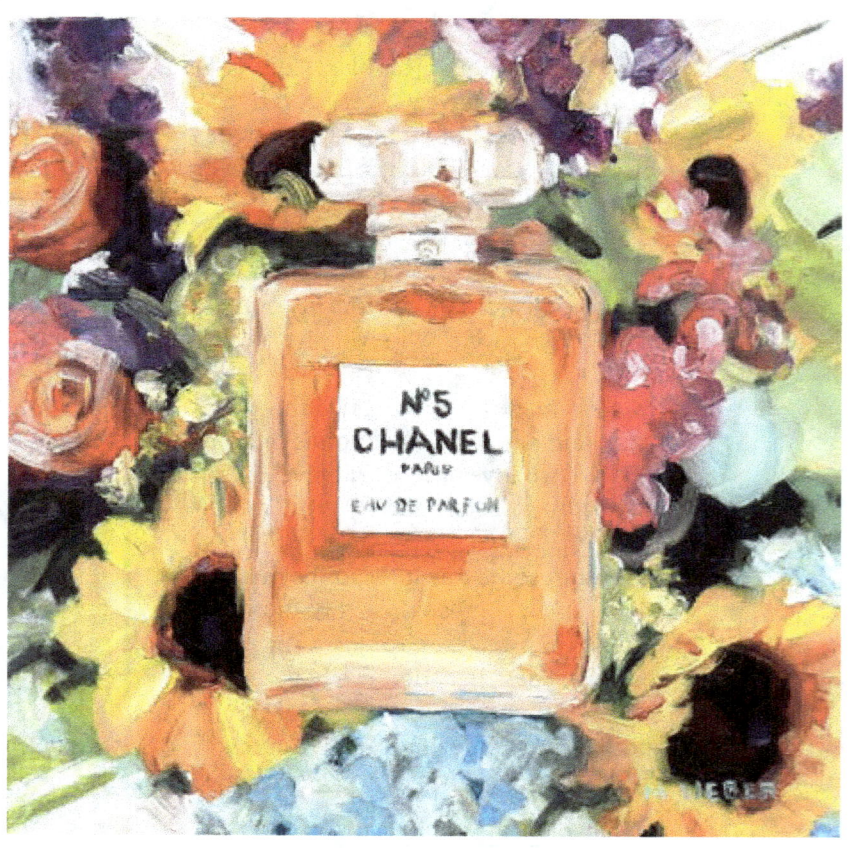

"For You" oil   **Merrill Weber**

ATTITUDE ADJUSTMENT
~ *Christine Ross*

Bursting through the doorway
grumbling
my tirade silently interrupted
by cinnamon
and apple tapping on my brain.

I realize she is baking.
wonder
if homemade dessert could possibly
end this crummy day
on a sweeter note.

Still grumpy I take up the rant
clanking
a wad of car keys on the marble slab
thunking leather bags
to the wooden floor.

Once more my voice is halted
I spy
linens, china, flickering candles, a bouquet
of fresh-cut garden stalks topped
with vivid velvet colors.

Soft and pungent floral
perfume
travels like a right hook into the hall
makes me dizzy, helps me lose my place
in the bad story.

So I skip over parts
pausing
my step and my story once again as I notice
she is humming, and she is smiling
in heels and pearls

and Channel No. 5.

I return her smile

grinning

like a fool while loosening my tie
forgetting a forgettable day
suddenly aware
I'd rather hear about hers.

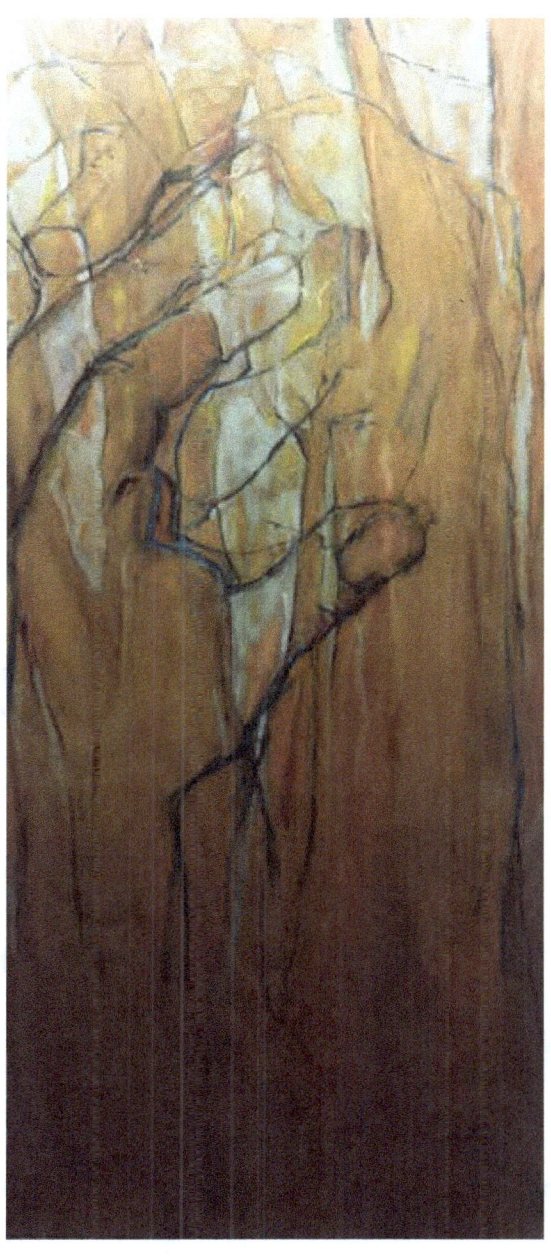

"Relinquish" oil　　　　　　　　　　　　　　　　Lauralynn White

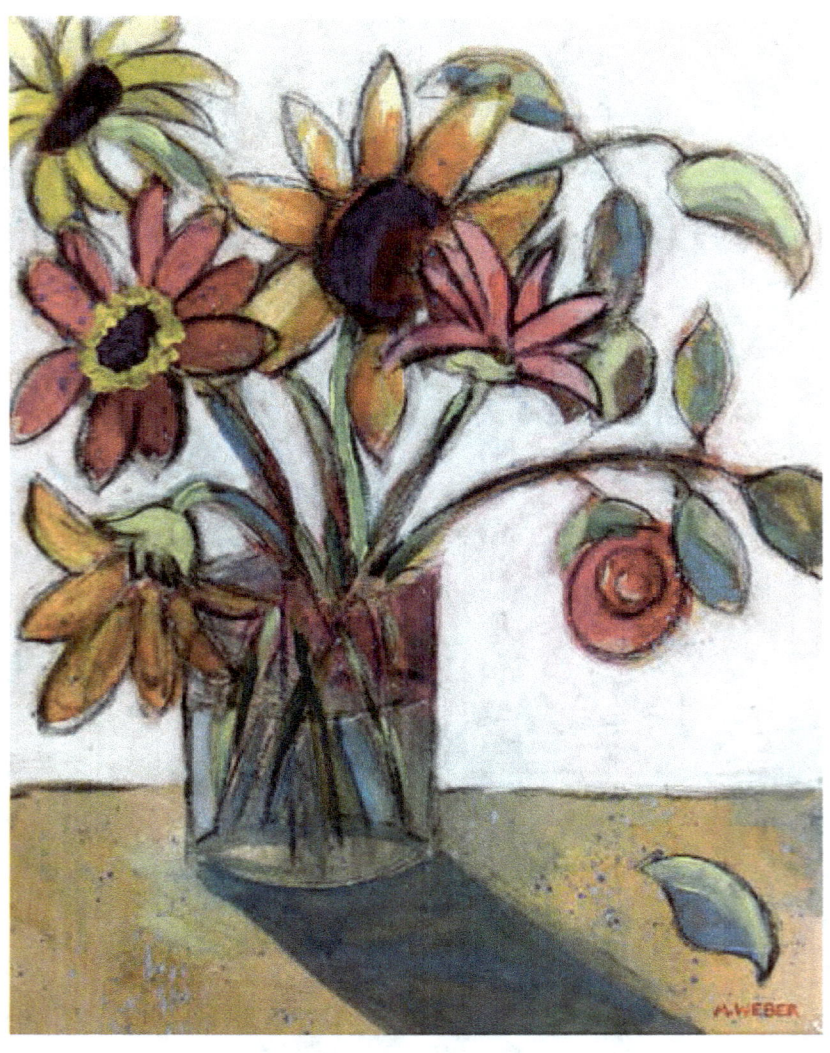

"Veranda View" oil   **Merrill Weber**

If One Would Just Take the Time
~ Ashley Rupert

It only takes one
Person to demonstrate
Thoughtless compassion to
Another, to rekindle the childlike
Trust, naive hope, and whimful actions
Based on the dormant past.

Simple acts that are
Passed off as a burden
For another to pick up
Our slack and pay for our
Sins, can be transformed into
Sympathy, if one would just
Take the time,

To stop thinking of oneself
As the sole being with a
Developing soul, a beating heart, an overworked brain and
See us all as human beings who
Hurt and grieve, lash out and regret,
Starve themselves to
feed the dreams they dare not
Share with the common or familiar.

If we turn our backs
To provide support for one to
Lean against in times of challenge,
Maybe then we'd be able to
Recline on the backs of others.
Maybe then, our back would not
Be so stiff from postures of attention
And constant watchfulness.
Our eyes, less frantic with sleep deprivation
And paranoia that stirs us from the dreams
Our hidden child so desperately brings back into sight
As we sleep away the stresses of the current day
Week, month, year- so easily avoided if one
Would just take the time.

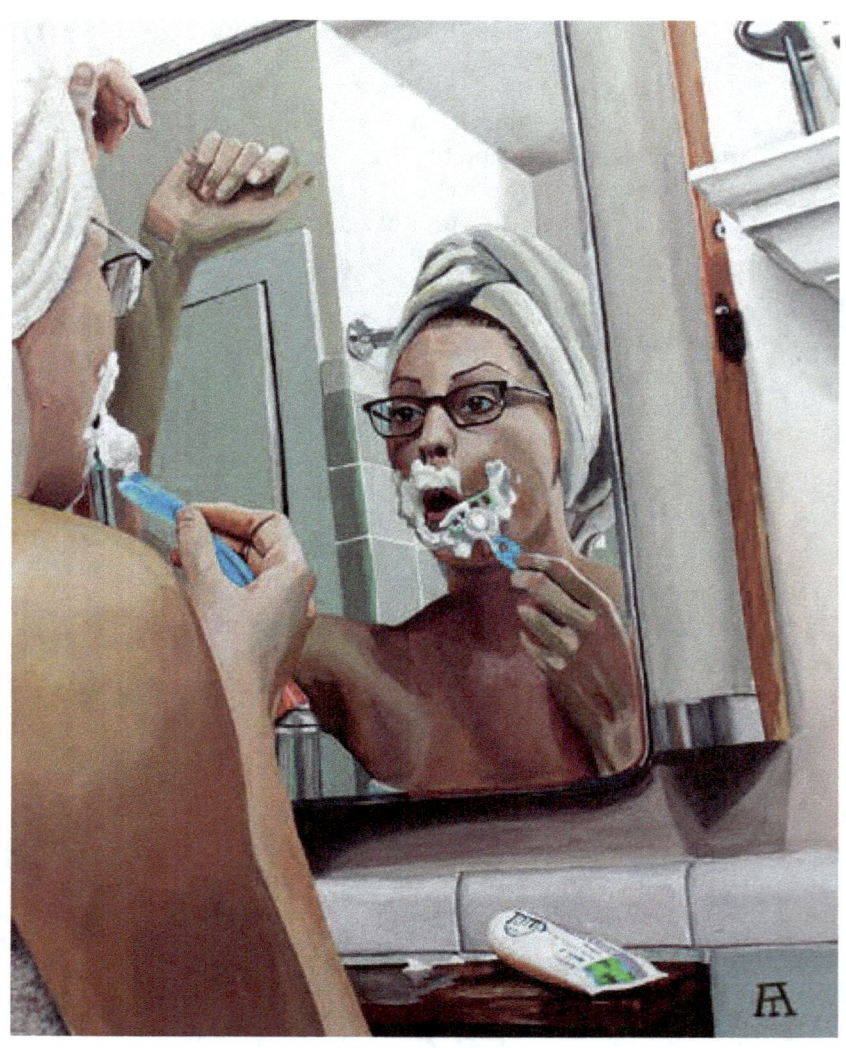

"Standards of Beauty" oil   *Angela Izzo*

More Than a Mere Reflection
~ *Ashley Rupert*

The mirror reflects
No portions of substance
Nor ounces of love and life
And provides no encouragement,
No warmth or passion
Of motherly praises or advice.

It shows not
The sentiment of character with
Which others discern
And does little to brag
Of your beauties and virtues,
The boasting of which you deserve.

The mirror reflects
No light of flattery
Nor enlightens the soul of shame
But shadows the mind
With doubt and humility
To limn body and soul as same,

Allowing vices and virtues
To mingle in folly
And disguise the beautiful truth
That body and soul are not the same,
And your reflection could
Never be you.

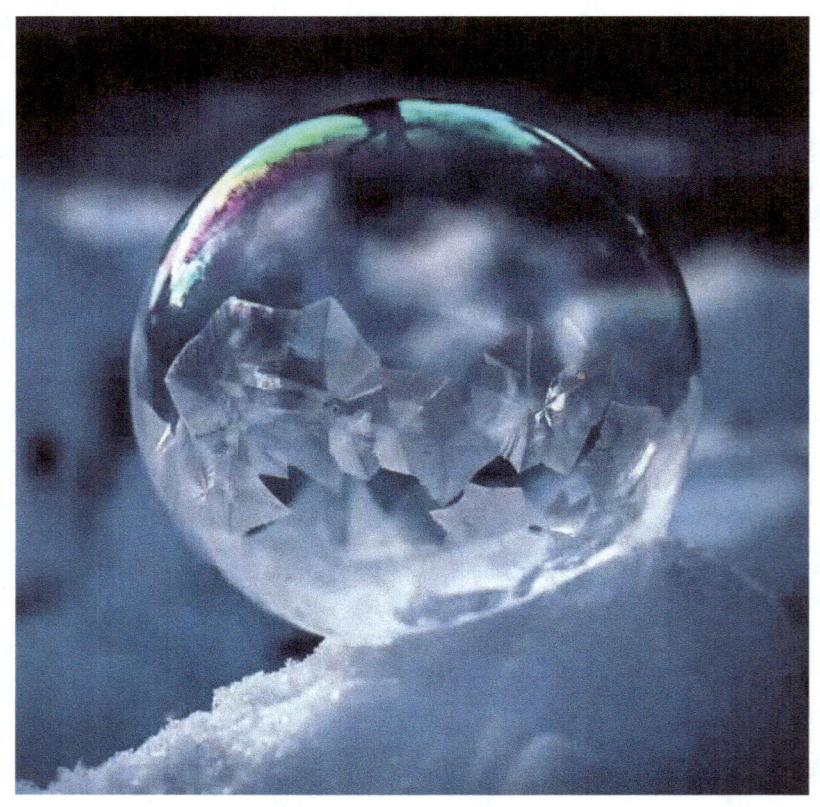

"Ice Bubble II" photo   **Rachel Conrad**

First Snow

~ *Michael Schiffman*

Heading west on the sinuous,
ominous turnpike. A brief getaway
to Wright's Falling Water.

Early November. Snow and cold
in the forecast. Sign of the climate
reckoning that lies ahead.

Southwestern Pennsylvania coal country.
Dreary towns plunked below the gorgeous
Laurel Highlands. The House a simple or a complex
wonder ensconced in this landscape as if found.
The rocks, the trees, the water. A situate dream.

The snow began as we climbed to our next stop.
Blinding snow. Stepped out of the car
only to retreat and drive on
to Kentuck Knob, the master's final work.

Two houses built for wealth and privilege
above the farms and mines.

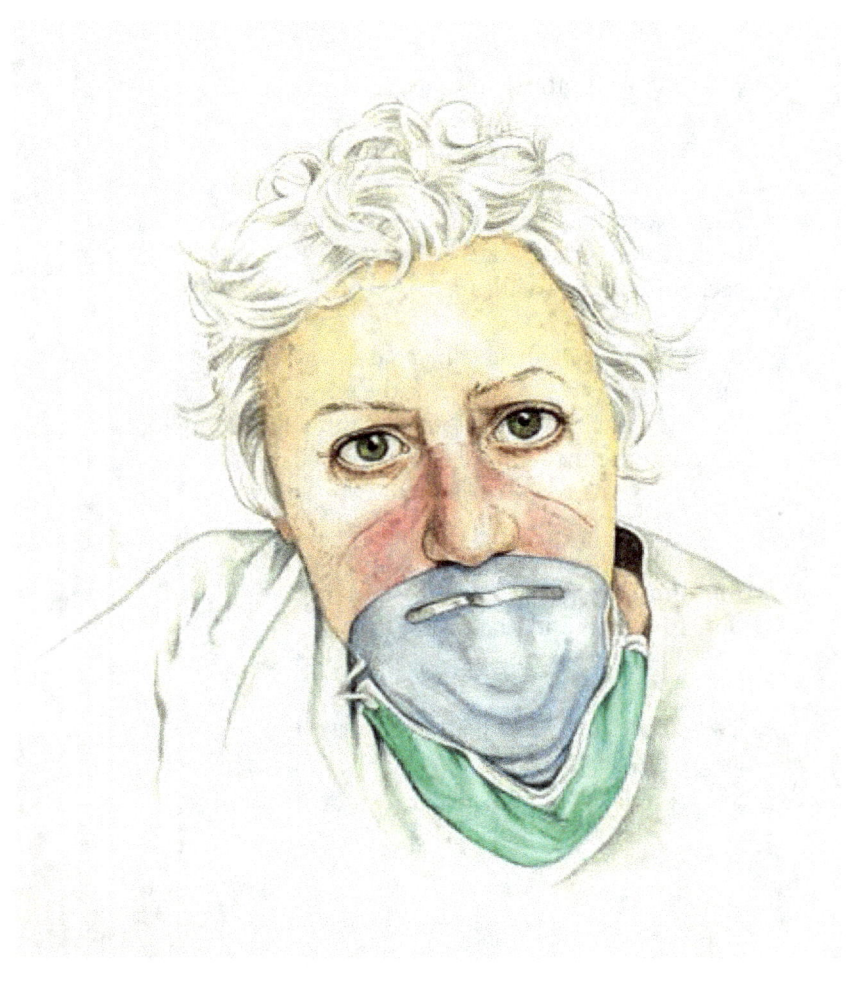

"Denise" watercolor   *Amanda Condict*

WHAT IS A PANDEMIC?
~ *Michael Schiffman*

Seventy-seven years on planet earth,
and I have yet to come into my own.
But now the pandemic has arrived, hidden
behind the grey clouds that sully each passing day.

Soon enough the dead will be lying in heaps
on macadam playgrounds, their weight
an illusory protest against implacable time.
What solace can there be?

Surely, the existential thesis has
been brought down from its philosophical
perch as isolation, face masks written
into law, infection resisting arrest. .

Don't be troubled. Nothing has changed.
And everything has been altered. Life and death,
the boring, heart-rending, unchangeable
carousel that reeks of humanity-and of spring flowers.

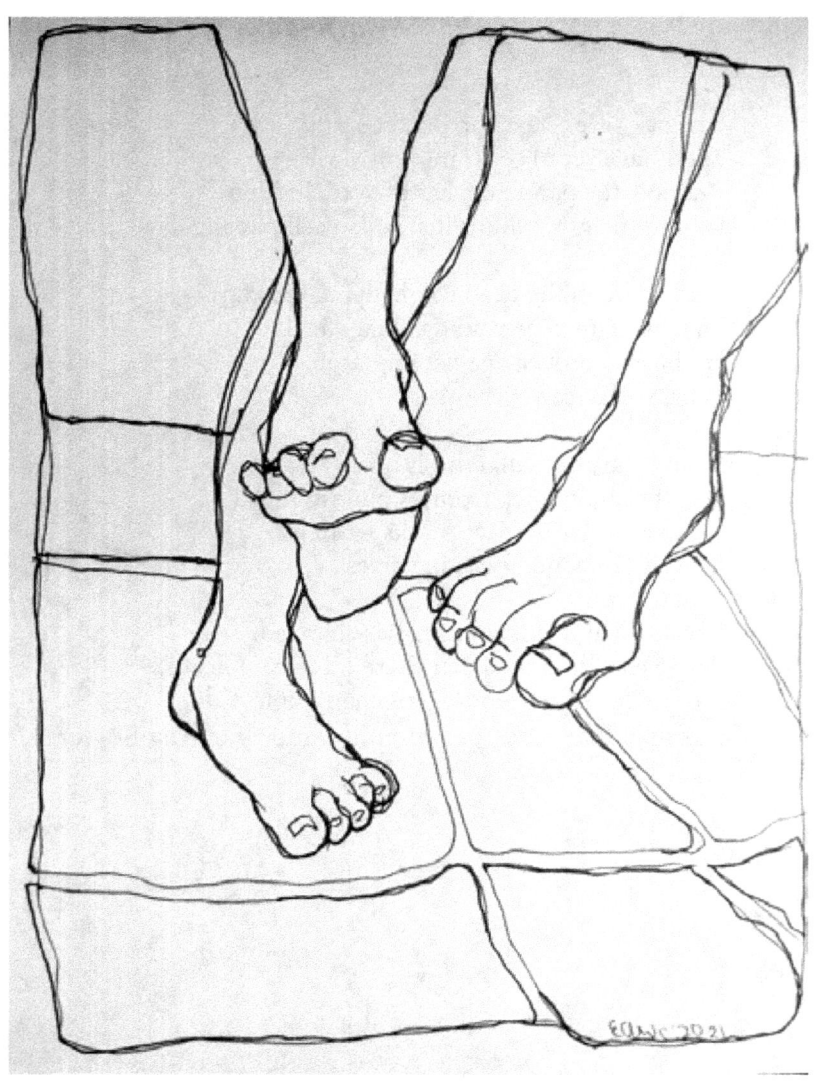

"Leg Drawings" ink   *Anne Chase*

BARE FEET
~Sandra Seaman

Bare feet on sunny sidewalks
running soles slapping
roots of ancient oaks
tilting cement slabs
glittered with a child's gems

Leaping over cracks
don't break
your mother's back

Never again as free
or as rich as I was then

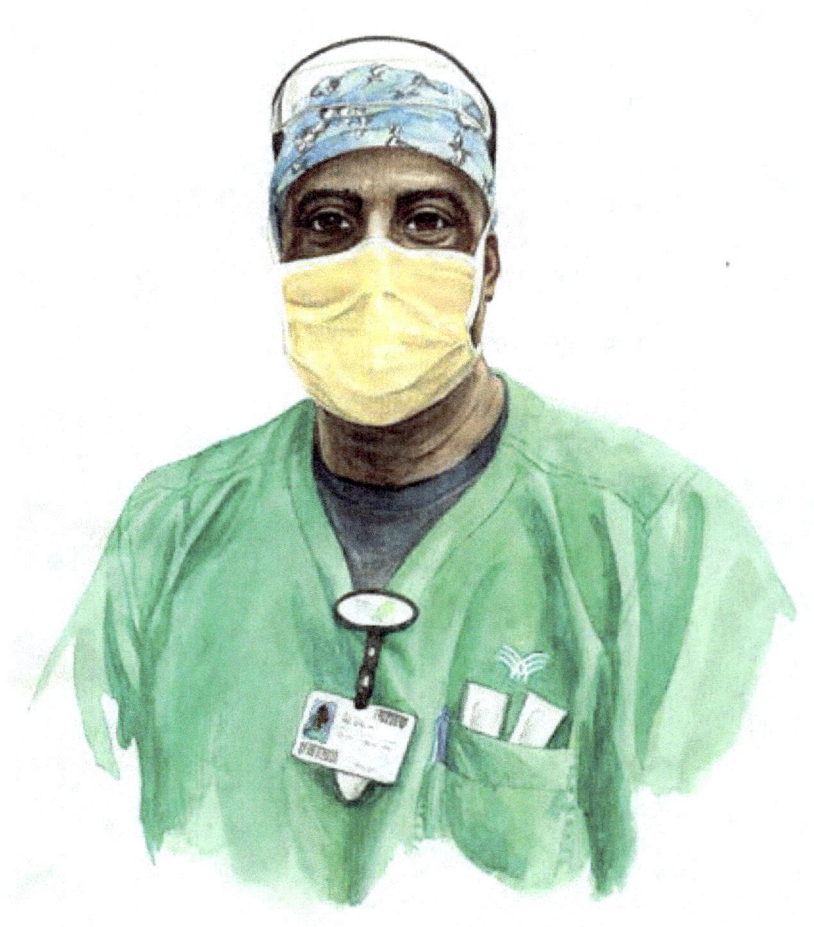

"Fred" watercolor   *Amanda Condict*

Light at the End of the Tunnel
~ *Sandra Seaman*

Virtual
Punxatawny Phil
groundhog days

Gluten free peanut butter and jelly
stevia sweetened chocolate chip
fear of apocalyptic annihilation
Bernie Sanders in mittens meme days

Up close and personal
with my inadequacies

nothing in
nothing out days

Pfizer Moderna Johnson and Johnson
65 and over
95 percent effective days

Hospital corridor
folding chairs spaced 6 feet apart
waiting for vaccine to thaw
skin bared
from winter coats
shot-in-the-arm
stirrings of hope days

All out of struggling
just wanting to sit
and be
days

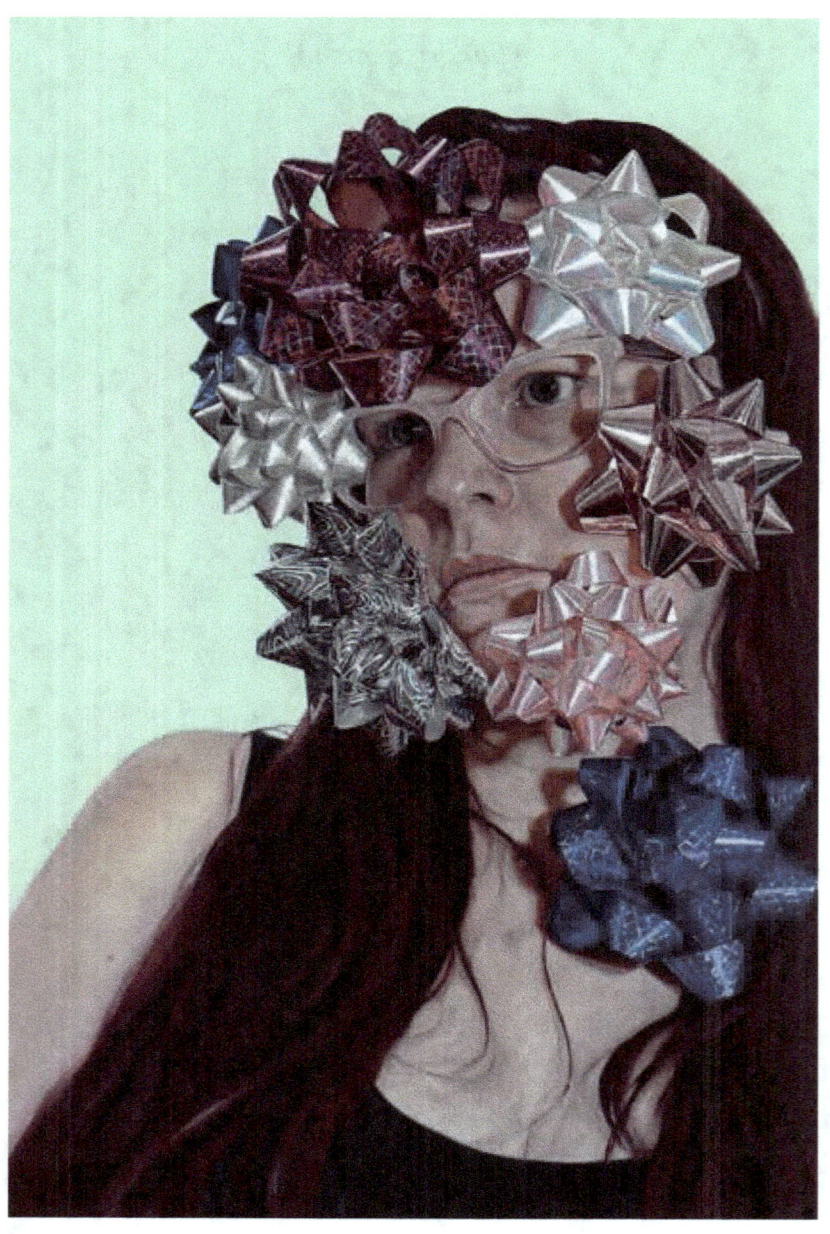

"The Celebrator" oil   *Hilary Swingle*

No Gifts Please!
~Jane Stahl

In the beginning: He made me laugh. He sang loudly, passionately—never in tune and usually with words he made up. Playing Scrabble he'd confidently create sentences to convince us that the unusual word he offered was legitimate.

The very first thing I remember about Paul when I met him was his humor. That humor found its way into what I call our "gifting" history. It's unique.

Our first gifts to one another pre-marriage were the romantic kind, but romance didn't last. Year #1 he bought me snow tires. Ten years later, my gift was a microwave. Practical gifts, for sure, Not funny, though.

The humor started the year he went into business, the year Amy was born, the year we had no income stream. We were living on borrowed money and, with a new business and a new baby, neither of us had money or any free time to shop.

Like minds: That Christmas I ordered 2 cute inexpensive soap dishes from a catalogue to have something—anything—to wrap. What a surprise on Christmas morning to open 2 bars of cute decorative soap he'd picked up at the local drug store on his way home on Christmas Eve.

(Forty years later we were still "in sync": one Christmas morning we surprised each other with replacement toilet seats.)

Art? Several years later—still financially strained, while we hated that our Buick Skylark lost a hubcap, we were loathe to spend the $25 to replace it. But the spirit of gift-giving provided the needed rationale: I gifted him with a hubcap for Christmas. So pleased, he hung it on the wall for about a month as a piece of art.

While buying it at the time was an extravagant and nonessential purchase during the early years of his business, that hubcap became for us what gifting was all about—surprise and fun—an out-of-the box conversation piece. And totally appreciated!

Bigger and Better: Another of Paul's favorite gifts was the enlarged trashcan service I ordered. Being a bit compulsive, he struggled and groaned each week the night before garbage day making sure everything fit neatly into the ordinary-sized trashcan that our trash service provided. Stressed as he was in running his business, he didn't need to be stressed over trash, so I had our service enhanced with a super-sized receptacle. Garbage night found Paul smiling! "Merry Christmas, Honey!"

They did what? On his 30th birthday, I invited his work friends to a party in our home. I was pregnant that year. They brought a stripper to the party as his gift. I don't recall inviting any of them ever again!

Caught begging: On our 10th anniversary he brought me flowers, perfume, and candy, hoping I'd return to work (and a paycheck) after my maternity leave ended.

My turn: After he sold his business and took a 2-year sabbatical from working, I gave him a potted plant, deodorant, and a Snickers bar for our 25th anniversary hoping he'd opt to rejoin the work force!

Win-win: One Mother's Day I presented him with a card that had a lovely message that expressed how I hoped he felt about me as the mother of his children. I included a present that I wanted him to give to me and wrapped it. The night before Mother's Day, I asked him to sign the card—which he happily did along with a smile and a "thank you" for saving him the time and effort shopping for me.

Tools: One Christmas I gifted him with a dozen nail clippers that he could strategically place around the house to have one always handy. It's time for another set: he has no idea where they are.

50 at 50: On his 50th birthday, I gave him 50 bars of soap, 50 rolls of toilet paper, 50 paper towels, among 50 other things he found practical and valuable. Clams and raisin drop cookies were included in the 50's collection!

60--Friends with benefits: On his 60th birthday, I bought and wrapped 60 items of all sorts of things he loved—mostly Clorox cleaning products—and had them available for his friends to give him throughout his birthday week at the local "greasy spoon" that he visited each morning for coffee or breakfast. Photos with those friends presenting him with the gifts were part of the celebration along with a photo album I then created to memorialize the birthday! He hated all the attention and made me promise never to do that again!

For the gambler: A few Christmases ago I rounded up all the turkey wishbones we'd saved over the years and wrapped a dollar bill around one of the "legs," suggesting that he invite friends to "make a wish" and whoever got the larger part of the bone won the $1. (Paul's a "regular" at our local casino; I figured he'd enjoy the "rush" of the gamble.)

For Fashion's Sake: Another Christmas I surprised him with a handsome wool overcoat so that he wouldn't need to wear his ugly, but warm, down coat to formal affairs. He soon figured out that his gift was really a gift to me: a few weeks before, I'd purchased my own formal winter coat and boots. I wanted us to look good—together!

"Nice Presentation, Honey": One year he'd admired a sport coat at our local men's store but deemed the item too expensive. "Not spending that kind of money on me!" he'd declared. Of course, I returned to the store without him and bought it. But it was the presentation that became the fun part.

The presentation happened while we were getting ready for a church service on Christmas Eve. Realizing his own sport coat was looking shabby, he asked our son if he could borrow *his* sport coat for the service. With a wink, I directed Jeff to where I'd stored the new coat that I'd bought to give to Paul the following morning. Paul, thinking it was Jeff's coat when he opened the zippered protective covering, enjoyed the surprise I'd created when he recognized what was now *his* new coat: "Nice presentation, honey," he said—quoting a line from a TV commercial that was running regularly that year.

By his 70th birthday, I gave him exactly what he wanted: nothing!

Squeaky wheel! One of my recent favorite gifts to Paul was inspired by his obsessive attention to detail. Every time he wore a particular shirt, he complained that the buttons were too white. They stood out against the shirt's dark brown plaid.

He liked the shirt and wore it often in company; yet every time he wore it, he complained—even to the same people: "What was the designer thinking?" he'd ask. So, right before Christmas when the shirt was in the wash, I replaced all the buttons with khaki-colored ones and wrapped it up as his Christmas gift. He's happier with it now, and he enjoys telling the story!

Treasure Hunt: This past Christmas I found items of cookware, plates, and drinking glasses he'd been wanting to replace. Some of the original items had been purchased 40 years ago and, despite his shopping and mine over many attempts over many years, replacements seemed nowhere to be found.

Undeterred, I hunted on e-bay and located the exact pieces. I also bought a replacement for a pair of shoes he purchased recently but hadn't been enjoying. Because he refuses to own more than one pair of shoes at a time, I made the puchase for him and ordered his preferred style.

But, again, the presentation of these gifts was part of the fun. Knowing how he hates receiving gifts, I told the kids that this year their dad was the focus of my gifting. He had the most gifts to open, but *they* would have the pleasure of opening them for him. He enjoyed watching them; I enjoyed his surprise and delight that I'd found the exact items he'd been wanting.

And—to top off my pleasure--with one gift left to open, he said, "Now if only you'd been able to find those plates I like." Yup, the last gift was those exact plates. I'll remember his smile, one that's increasingly hard to come by in recent years—especially at any gifting occasion—for a long, long time.

The Ultimate—for me: Finally, my favorite: I've had a great time over the years finding gifts that surprise and fill a desire or need or provide a fun and funny presentation opportunity. But shopping of any kind is work for Paul. He decided to quit shopping one Christmas Eve when he went shopping for gifts for us and came home with a new leather jacket for himself —something that he always wanted.

Today Paul does his shopping for all of us in 15 minutes at the local bank for gifts of cold cash, but years ago he gave me something I always wanted: an inground pool in my own backyard.

The Ultimate—for him: My gift to him that Christmas was a box of over 50 Christmas bows with a note saying that anytime he felt he *should* be finding a gift for me—for Christmas or birthday, Mother's Day or Valentine's Day, he need only throw a bow in the pool to remind me that he'd already given me *my* gift of a lifetime. I think that colorful box of bows has been one of Paul's favorite things—signifying a joy for both of us forever!

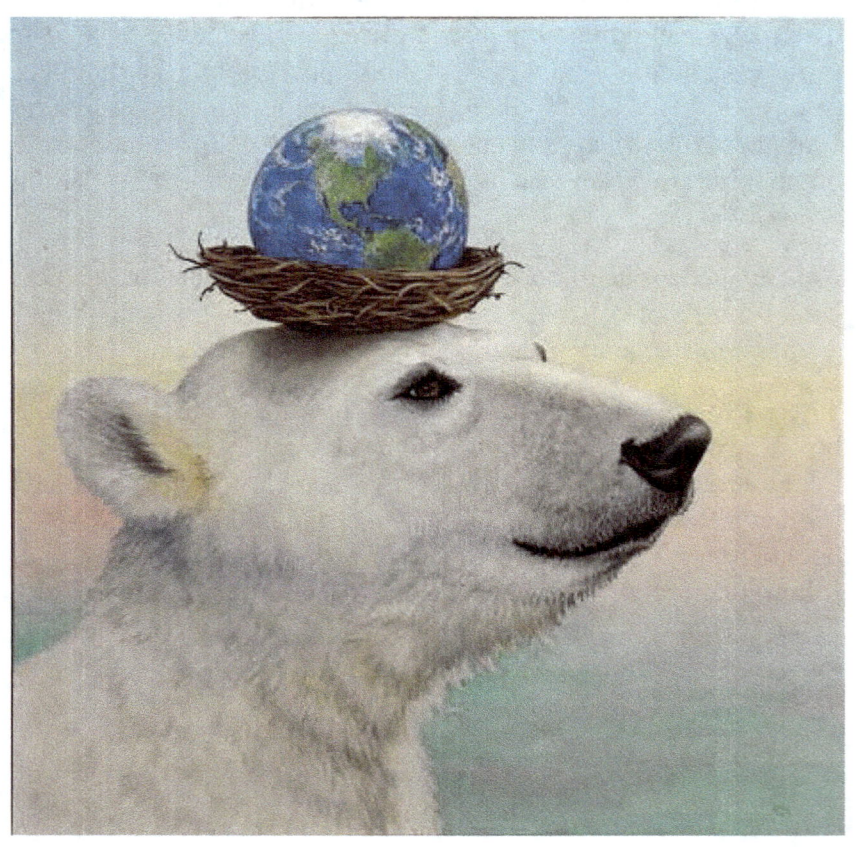

"In the Balance" oil   **Kathryn E. Noska**

A Greeting

~ *Jane Stahl*

Sunlight warms the glass,
Tags the crystal watch face on my wrist, reflecting
Rainbow gleams to dance around the spiraled stair.

Embraced in solar warmth,
Relaxed in friendly humors, the
Cold,
Rejecting faces
melt away.

I'm home.

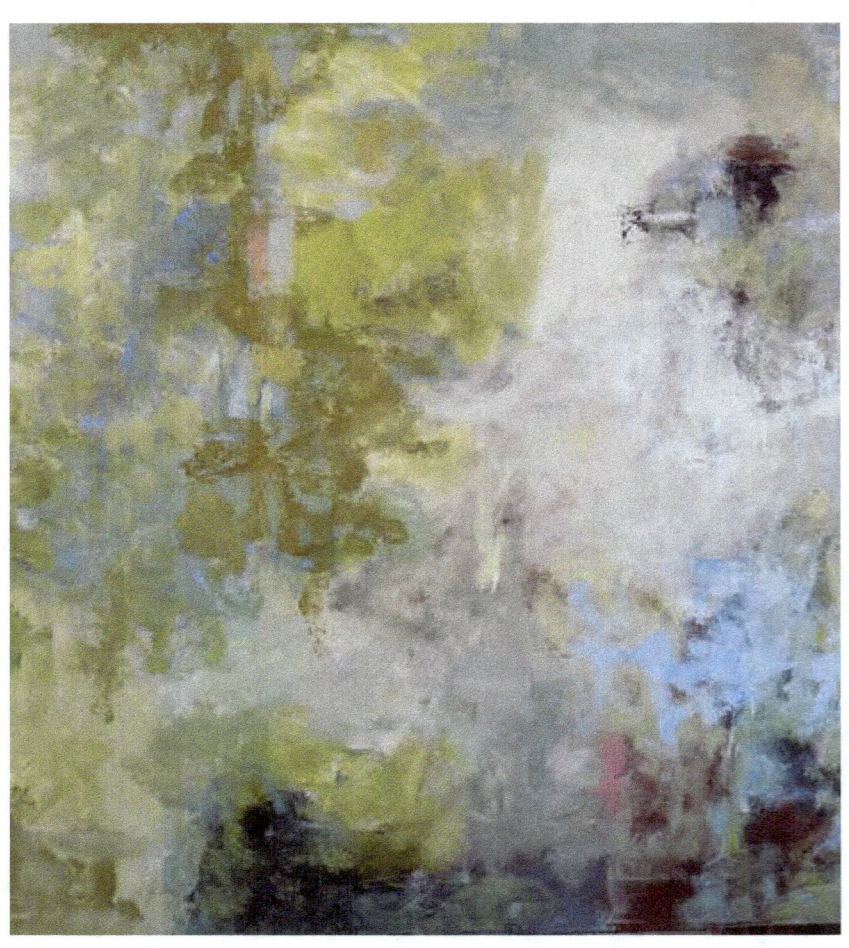

"Koi Pond" *acrylic*   ***Marilyn Fox***

BOTTOM TO THE TOP
~JD Stahl

I'm in love with space.
Since we first tied the knot.
Day dream dip in my memories.
Causal mate guiding me.
Zero point creations.
Ionic sensations.
Action and rest.
Infinitesimal. The best.
From here to the end.
Mental math. Passed test.

Through the black.
Out the white.
Holes and time.
Her way is mine.
From day, our night.
Non-physical house of light.
Never fear. Never fight.
Absolutely all right.

Toroidal contraptions,
Like apples and seeds.
Flawless love and affection.
Nothing to prove—no need.
You pay her attention.
No competition or greed.
She brings Nature to her knees.
Nothing compares to her sea.

She's particle number one.
I'm the father of the axes.
Tall vertical direction
Lignin likened to humanity.
Learned language of our Sun.
Photosynthetic affinity.
Channeling through humanity.

Invisible key. Harmonic frequency.

Singular organization,
Astral masks—taken faces.
A remote, non-local nation.
She wins all the races.
Silver-corded fascination.
Fiber-laced space case.
Shape-shifting reputation.
Canal-fluid hallucination.
From bottom to the top.
It's already got.

Precious metal confetti.
She's my abominable ascension.
Passionate tastes of infinity.
The absolute connection.
Broken torrent of information.
Lack of concentration.
A black coffee strange brew.
Surfing for the clue.

Plasma rich nervous zoo.
Right here inside me, waking.
Whatever fluid works for you.
Instant energy. No waiting.
What's true is true.
My imagination, forever creating.
She's the flame I'm breathing.
My ventricle, beating.
I'm her king. She's my queen.
My density destiny.

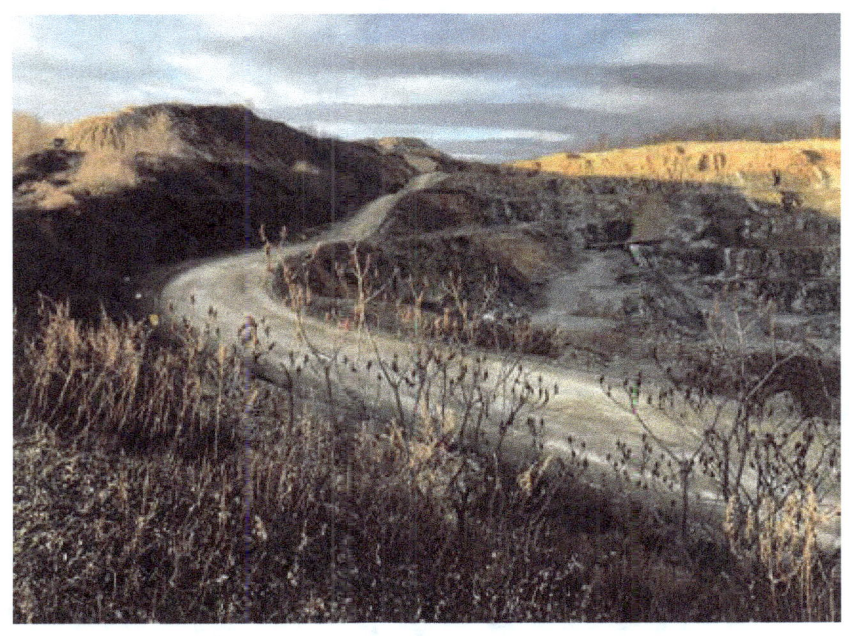

"A Road Less Traveled" photo *Nicole Johnson*

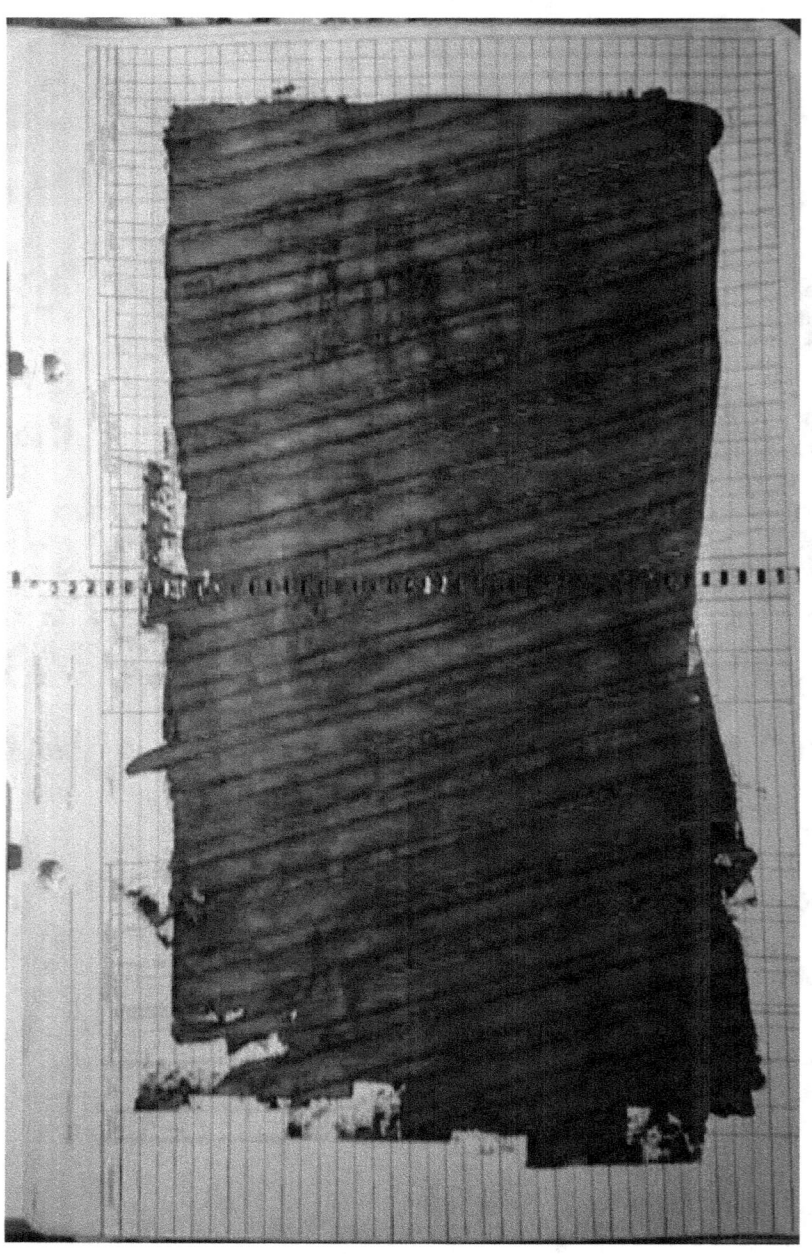

"Untitled" drawing   **Ron Schira**

Inspiration

~ *JD Stahl*

There is a place which cannot be hidden.
A flame never to be extinguished.
This light that shall never darken.
Reflects upon everything that you love.

Made of material that never shall perish.
A sacrifice, for which you'd be willing to die.
Birthing passion, never to be exceeded.
Exposing all of your fears into lies.

Every pain will retreat in its presence.
Hate and spite will run from its gaze.
All rivers of life stream from its balance.
Those who seek it shall always be saved.

It's purity defines the words of the ages.
No sadness could ever match its relief.
Death, itself, even bows to reverence.
It breaks all temporal rules known in time.

A joke to anything held in your senses.
Priceless, exceeding all diamonds and gold.
Dedicated to your greatest devotion.
Heavier than the strongest hands could hold.

This gift that we were all given each birth,
Is at the root of all of creation.
The answer which all seekers will seek.
Unconditional love is our only salvation.

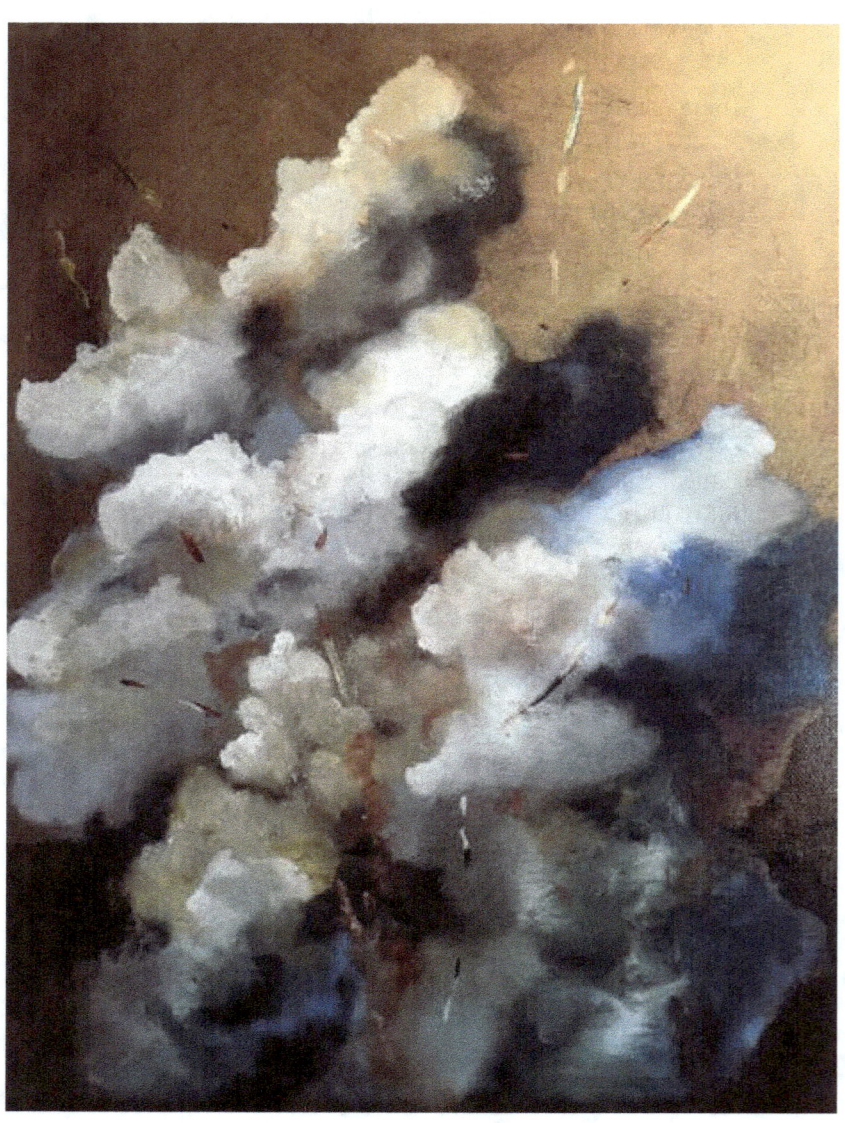

"Vesuvius, 2021" oil   *Daniella Yacono*

Humha: The Monster

~ *Taku,* known as *VaChikepe,*

Because they didn't like me
And because they didn't
Want anything to do
With me!

They told me that...
Their life was full of "Humha"

Humha: The monster!

The monster that was going to
Eat me! If ever, I come closer
To them!

They kept themselves to
Theirselves and pushed me
Away! They closed their doors
To my face and they also closed
Their doors behind my back
and they shouted...

"Go! Go! Go! Don't come here
Humha with eat you! There is
A monster here! The
Monster will eat
You!"

Hence, they kept themselves to
Themselves But! Deep inside
My heart, I knew there was
No Humha in their lives!
If there was Humha
In their lives,
Humha was
Going to
Eat...
Them first before me!

Yes I resisted and tried to push
Myself in their lives! Yes they
Overpowered me and used

Force to disengage me
And disconnect me!

Why did they do that?

They saw me different from them!
They didn't like my energy levels
And I was simply a disturbance
In their lives, useless and
Totally incapable of
Comprehending
Anything!

Or they simplify didn't have time
For me! They were too busy
Addressing different
Issues of their life!

I guess that is the reason, why
They created the "Humha:
The Monster" concept

...Against me!

In this life! Is there a "Humha
The Monster," somewhere

Out there: In a small
Box, but preparing
To eat us all?

Or we have lived with "Humha
The Monster" all the days of
Our lives, like the air that
We breathe!

But only in our sphere of
Ignorance?

I stand! To ask...

" Humha: The Monster"

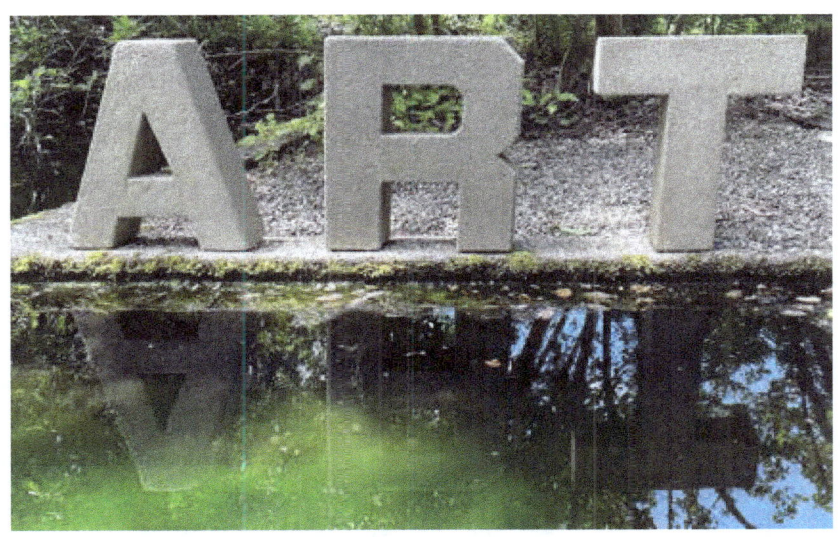

"ART" concrete sculpture   *Jerry Kott*

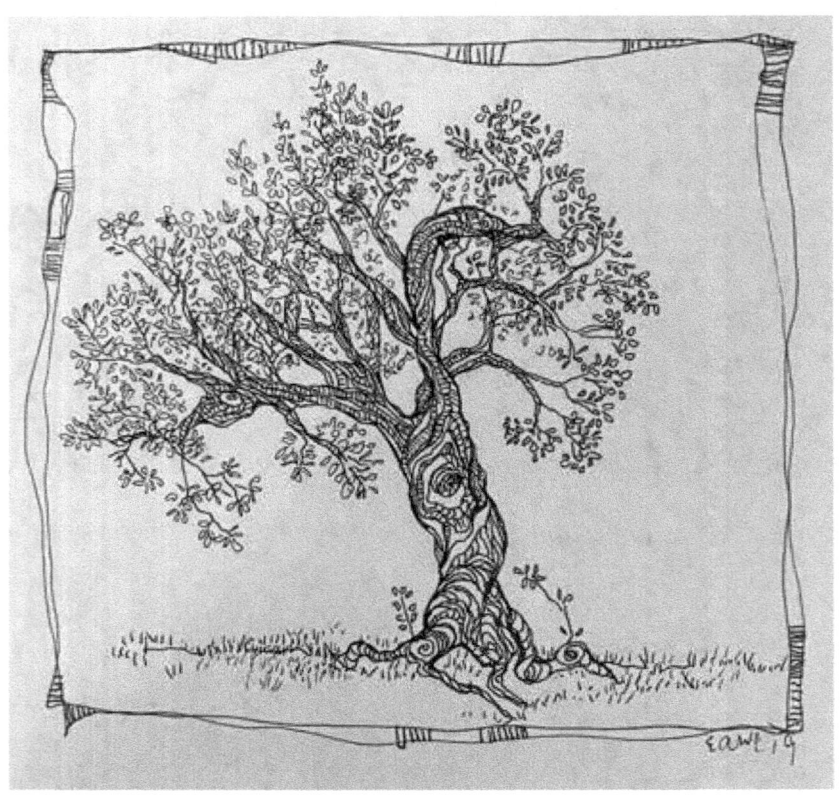

"Winding Tree" ink *Anne Chase*

SAN MATEO 1943

~ *Ted Thomas*

Dorniers, Spitfires, Heinkels, and Hurricanes
Swoop and dive
Like gulls over a fishing boat
In aerial combat
In a boy's bedroom
In our ten-year-old imaginations
We were the young men in those airplanes
That hung from the ceiling
That summer Demetrius Leonardus joined the Air Force
While his brother George and I hid among the dancing leaves
Of a neighboring pin oak tree
Embraced by the earth of that summer of '43
His letters left a trail across the map from flight training
To bombing practice
To a refueling stop in Iceland
And finally to East Anglia England
Our leafy hideout in the treehouse concealed the approaching car
It rolled to a stop
An officer emerged
Entered the Leonardus home
We returned to our comic books
The officer departed quietly
And the car pulled away from the curb
After what seemed like hours but only minutes
Mrs. Leonardus came out arms full of the aircraft
That once hung from Demetrius' bedroom
She set the pile aflame in the middle of the street
And returned to the home in silent grief
For three months never speaking a word.

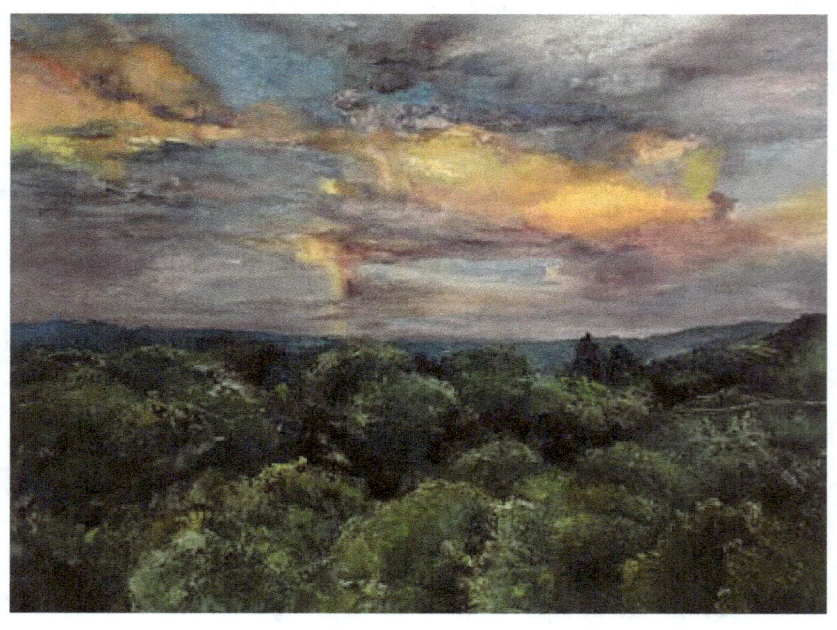

***"Treescape"* acrylic** *Joanne Moy*

Sunday Morning

~ Ted Thomas

Sunday School is out!!!
Boyhood energies burst through the church door
Into the dazzling sunlight of El Camino Real
That ribbon of highway that threads south from San Francisco
Bordered by towering eucalyptus casting long shadows
On the heavy traffic passing through Burlingame
To an eight-year-old boy
A eucalyptus is more than a tree
It's a source of pleasure every step of the way home
Its seed pods are soft and swollen with a pungent oil
When a boy's heel lands on one the oil drenches shoes and sidewalk
One's mind is concentrated on the game
Leap further land squarely and keep count of the hits
Consequences await as always
The acrid odor will go home with my shoes
Oh! To hear again those shrieking sounds of motherhood
But not right now while I am crushing seed pods under foot
Raising a stench
Sudden awareness of silence
No traffic nothing moving
People gathered around cars stopped in traffic lanes
Car doors open radios blaring
I walked closer to one of the silent clusters of alarmed faces
The announcers voice rose above the din of exploding bombs
Attacking aircraft and gunfire
Strange names of unknown places broke through his speech
Hawaii Scolfield Barracks Hickum Field Pearl Harbor Honolulu
Midday in California 7 a.m. in Honolulu this beautiful Sunday morning

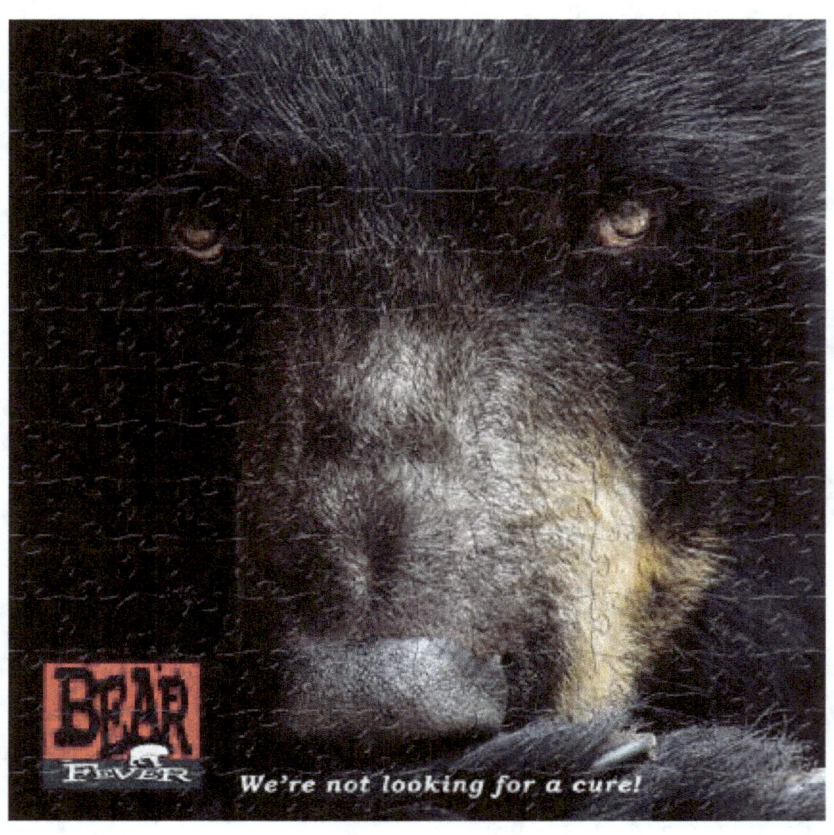

"Bear Fever Puzzle"   *Available Only at Studio B*

JIGSAW PUZZLES ARE MY ADDICTION
~ *Nelvin Vos*

I really like jigsaw puzzles. They are not only one of my favorite things; they are my addiction for I can't live well without them. That realization has become even more clear during this time of self-isolation of the pandemic. My eighty-eight-old being has found consolation, comfort, and great enjoyment from my puzzles.

As a child, I had many jigsaw puzzles and completed them again and again. In my college years and teaching career, puzzle-making went into a kind of eclipse. But during that time, at least one puzzle would preoccupy me during winter, especially during the holidays or when a snowstorm would occur.

A few years ago, a friend gave me a wooden jigsaw puzzle from Liberty Puzzles. I later became aware there are a number of companies who produce wooden puzzles.

I was even more hooked. The image was Vincent van Gogh's "Starry Sky." Now I own a dozen or so Liberty Puzzles – paintings of van Gogh and Vermeer (my ethnic Dutch background), a number of French Impressionists such as Monet, Manet, and Cezanne as well as more prosaic subjects as a brightly-colored fish or a lovely bouquet of flowers.

Several characteristics of these puzzles seduce me. From childhood on, the way to start a puzzle was to dump out all the pieces, turn them over, and sort them by identifying the side pieces and then construct these pieces as the frame. But that does not work in this new world of puzzle. About two-thirds of the side pieces have the usual straight edges but the rest are hidden, for example, a triangle piece in which one of the corners becomes part of the edge.

And then even more challenging are puzzles with no straight edges. The outline of the puzzle is the image itself, for example, the golden head of Pharaoh or a fish or a bird, all in dazzling color.

A special feature of all these puzzles are "whimsy" pieces. These pieces are created in the shape of objects: characters, animals or complex geometric figures. So one meets a bicycle, a rabbit, a pilgrim, or an intricate abstract pattern. Often these "whimsy" pieces are in keeping with the image of the puzzle. All very challenging and intriguing.

I enjoy going to the puzzle table after a day of facing words and more words at my computer or my desk or with a book or magazine. The day's frustrations are put aside in order to concentrate on these small pieces of wood. That's why I find puzzle-making a time of calmness and peace, especially in the evening.

PUZZLE-MAKING GIVES ME A SENSE OF ACCOMPLISHMENT

I begin with a pile of odds and ends, a world of chaos. And out of that chaos emerges, after much time and effort, a new creation. To finish a jigsaw puzzle is to experience a feeling of concrete and tangible completion similar to looking back at a newly-mown lawn or a freshly-weeded row of young vegetables. So many of our tasks such as parenting and teaching end in only occasional evidence which is tangible and specific. The rewards of puzzle-making are right there at the end.

Each of the characteristics which I have described above has become doubly important during this time of self-isolation. Puzzle manufacturers have experienced 30% increase in sales the past years. I have experienced both delays and shortages in my puzzle orders.

And when I began to do some research on this topic, I found there are psychological reasons for the mania right now. For the citations in the rest of this piece, I am indebted to Caroline Bologna, "Why Jigsaw Puzzles Are So Soothing And Addicting At This Time," Huffpost.com.

"While Covid-19 is associated with the lack of control and an unknown end, puzzles offer the opposite," said Michael Vilensky, a psychologist at Ohio State University's Wexner Medical Center.

"With a puzzle, with enough time and effort, we can control the outcome, know it will end, and experience a sense of relief and accomplishment when it is finished."

Karen Kavett, owner of a company which makes jigsaw puzzles up to 25,000 pieces, agrees that jigsaw puzzles are a great activity when the world feels out of control because the task is entirely within your power. She adds, "It's also an activity where you're assembling an item that already exists, rather than needing to expend mental energy to create something new."

Puzzles can provide a clear goal and sense of purpose in this time when people feel unable to map out future plans. Jenny Maenpaa, a New York City psychotherapist, writes that "doing a puzzle feels like working towards something bigger than your to-do list, which is especially alluring when meaningful action in quarantine can be hard to come by."

Patrick K. Porter, creator of BrainTap Technologies, has noted that there's a neuroscience component to this phenomenon. "The conscious mind is known as a servomechanism, meaning it is goal-striving. During quarantine, when we have no environmental changes from one day to the next, it can feel like we're living in Groundhog Day, as depicted in the Bill Murray movie. [Every day is a Blursday –nv] Jigsaw puzzles provide a challenge that gives this goal-seeking behavior an outlet. With each puzzle piece found, the puzzler gets a little bit of dopamine, which soothes the brain, and this reward then climaxes with the puzzle's completion."

Psychotherapist Maenpaa suggests that jigsaw puzzles are unique in the way they engage both the logical part of the brain (rationally fitting pieces together) and the creative side (envisioning the big picture of the completed work)

Porter has observed that our brains love patterns, but the uncertainty of the pandemic has disrupted our usual patterns of daily activities and left our minds seeking ways to fill that void. "In common times, the problem-solving part of our brain is active all day whether by navigating through traffic or working through a busy schedule

This is how our brains build and maintain neuroplasticity, the ability to stay flexible and active. Therefore, jigsaw puzzles are an excellent choice for people of all ages during quarantine, or any time."

And what could be a better bit of advice than that!

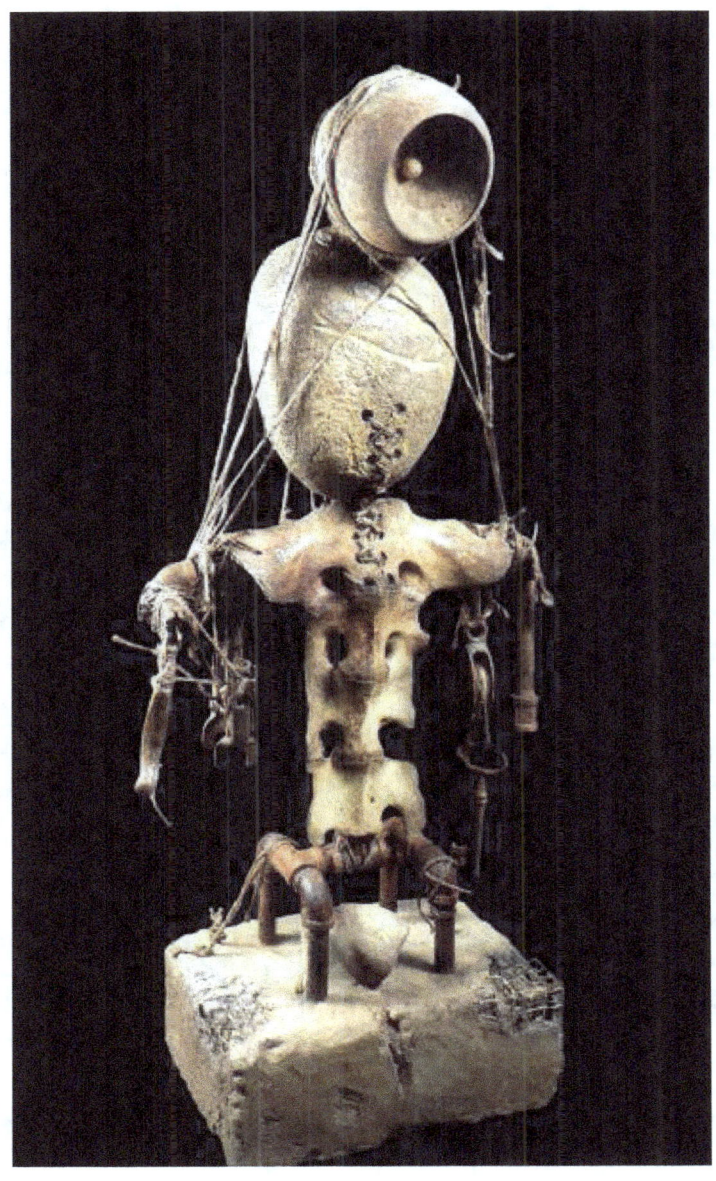

"Nightshade Hunter-Gatherer" assemblage   **Bob Hakun**

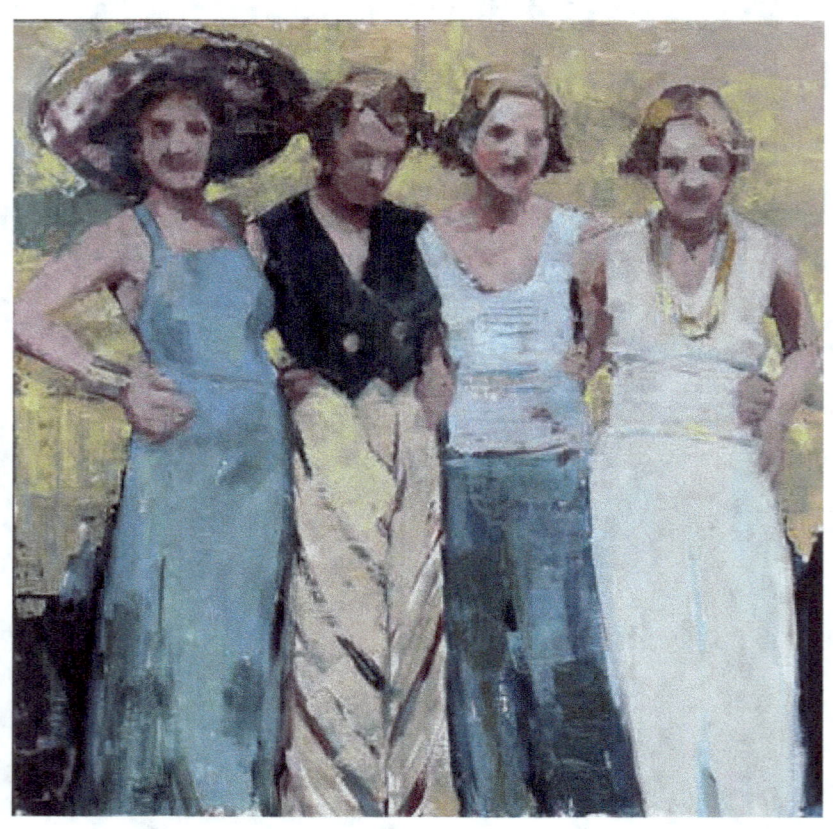

"Girls Club" oil   *Maryanne Buschini*

GIRLFRIENDS

~ *Aressa Williams*

Think about deep sadness. Multiply that feeling twenty times; that's the way I felt when I had a hysterectomy. Twenty-eight was too young for such a distressful operation. Large fibroid tumors defaced my womb. Although I was the mother of a son, I always expected to have other children once I got married. To make matters worse, the guy I loved liked me because "you can have boys." We broke up a month before my operation. He had a new girlfriend. Home recuperating, I had time to nurse my despair. Thoughts of suicide to escape unbearable suffering haunted me. But I had to live for my son. Mother was taking care of my five-year-old while I healed from the surgery.

My broken heart and anger with God made me cry off and on every day. I could not sleep nor eat. Why was God punishing me? I had friends who used abortions as birth control. I got pregnant once, had my baby, and used "the pill." I never had an abortion so why me? I did the right thing. Abject self-pity consumed me. Discouraged, I wondered how long the pain would last. What could I do to make the pain go away?

The second Saturday home from the hospital, four girlfriends knocked at my door. A surprise visit, all at the same time! They came bearing gifts. Gaynell gave me yellow carnations in a crystal vase. Dorothy handed me a bag of cinnamon buns, orange juice, and a *Cosmopolitan* magazine. Sarah was "special delivery," a colored drawing from my son and "a little change" in a white envelope from Mother. Harriette wanted to take me for a joyride in her new Pontiac Lemans. Who would believe four concerned companions visited simultaneously and nobody planned it? My weariness magically disappeared.

After hugs, I took a shower, put on a sundress I was saving for a party, combed my hair. The ladies opened the drapes for sunlight, straightened up the living room, cleaned the kitchen while I got myself together. Harriette jetted to a nearby deli to buy lunch for all of us. We sat around the walnut dining table, ate turkey clubs, slaw, chips inbetween sips of Pepsi. We talked about old times; (all friends since junior high school) Gaynell and Dorothy, hilarious storytellers, made me laugh until my side hurt. We planned an annual fall outing, a shopping trip to Reading, Pennsylvania. Three hours later, my friend-sisters wanted me to rest. They left me feeling cared for, valued, grateful. I slept well that night.

Girlfriends are joys forever. They help us to define who we are through common values, shared experiences, peer wisdom. Down in the gutter and kicked in the teeth? Best friends pull you up. No judgement, no criticism, no jealousy, no left-handed compliments. Real ones wish you well and appreciate you. Girlfriends are respectful, compassionate, generous, fun, thoughtful, safe path-partners. Beautiful!

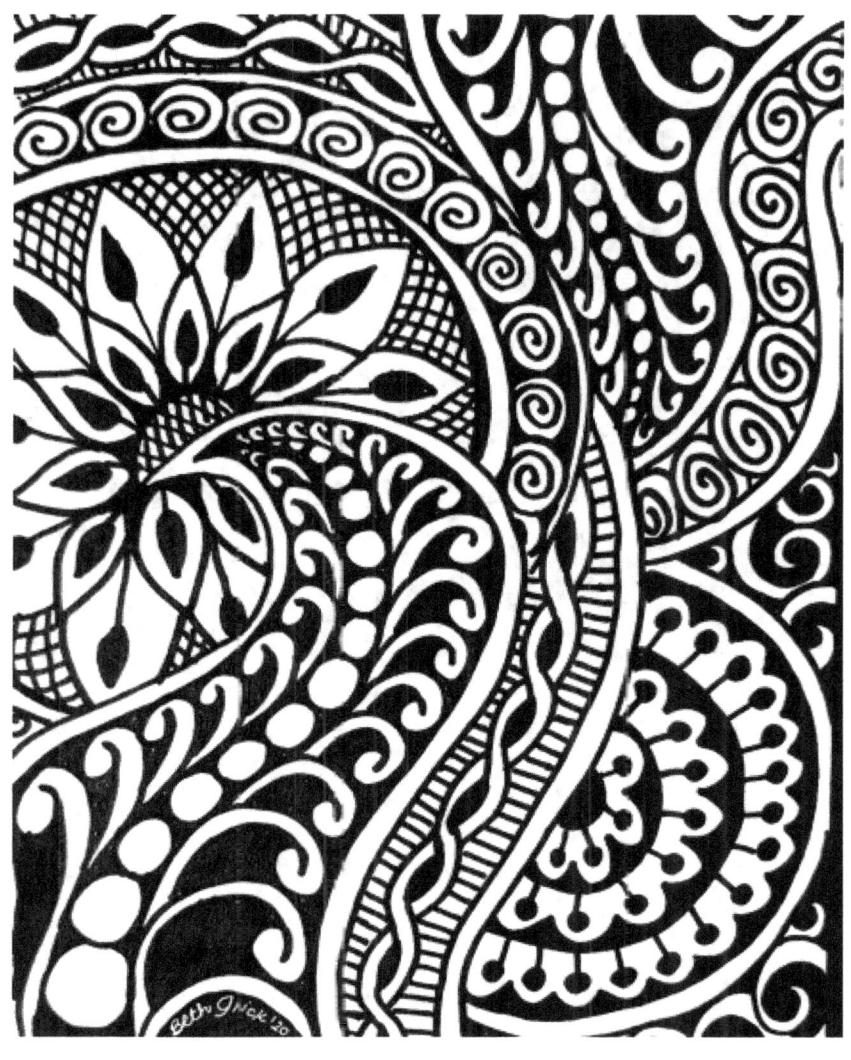

"Doodle Floral" ink — Beth Glick

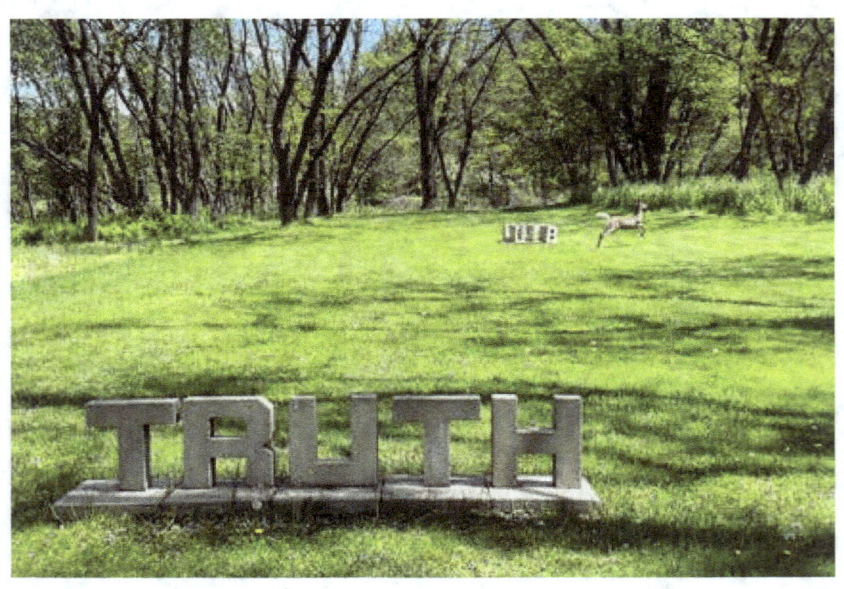

"TRUTH" sculpture   ***Jerry Kott***

My Favorite Things
~ *Sandra Williams*

Beauty, Goodness and Truth are not just a "few of my favorite things," but my very favorite and precious things in all the world. Although they are not "things," rather qualities or states of being, nevertheless, they are ubiquitously manifested in the material world, recognizable in people, places and things. I understand and experience them in so many ways, sometimes individually, sometimes intertwined in inextricable ways. I observe them all around me, sometimes unexpectedly hidden in a gesture, a word or a deed. I also feel them in my own thinking, feeling and will (i.e., mind, heart and actions). That this trinity exists affirms life and serves as inspiration, touchstones and guides.

The words of a song from *The Sound of Music* only begin to suggest the effects of my favorite things, *"When I'm feeling sad / I simply remember my favorite things / And then I don't feel so bad."* There is so much more than remembering and feeling better. Beauty, Goodness and Truth: each has the capacity to convey various levels of meaning and to engender gratitude and even joy, day to day and through a lifetime.

Beauty

In the poem "Tintern Abbey," William Wordsworth returns after five years to the banks of the River Wye in Wales. At the sight of the abbey and surrounding landscape, he realizes that, "These beauteous forms, / Through a long absence, have not been to me / As is a landscape to a blind man's eye." The scene had lived in him all those years, and was, "Felt in the blood, and felt along the heart; / And passing even into my purer mind." Beauty has, "no slight or trivial influence / On that best portion of a good man's life / His little, nameless, unremembered, acts / Of kindness and of love." And when recollected, "the heavy and the weary weight / Of all this unintelligible world/Is lightened."

Wordsworth's revelation describes how beauty affected him, and, as eloquent writers often do, also articulates our own experience. My recollections over the years of living in Florence, Italy—golden light falling on red tile roofs and ancient stone, tall cedars on azure hills, the green Arno, gardens and fountains, resounding church bells—have sustained me, as have experiences of beauty since: sunsets, spring blossoms, snowfall, sea meeting sky, Van Gogh sunflowers, my grandchildren's pure and shining faces. Beauty in the moment or remembered brings peace and joy and lightens the heavy and weary weight of the world. Things of beauty are, indeed, a joy forever!

Goodness

Under the umbrella of Goodness are many qualities to consider: ethics, honesty, civility, patience, kindness, compassion, integrity, actions and deeds for the common good. Goodness comes in many forms: Simple—paying it forward when the person ahead of you pays for your coffee at a Starbucks window. Or profound—as when Mahatma Gandhi instructed one of his distraught Hindu followers whose son was killed in a skirmish between Hindu and Muslim mobs: "Go and find an orphan child born of Muslim parents, adopt him as your own son, and bring him to worship Allah with the ideal of non-violence."

We do not always see Goodness when we most need to, as it is often compromised in personal, professional, religious and political dealings. It can be difficult to live up to the demands of Goodness, yet examples are all around us. We can also contribute in large and small, but significant ways for the benefit another soul or for the common good, fostering hope for and faith in humanity.

Truth

Truth is relative, it is said, which mostly refers to "our own truth," specific to us as individuals, having formed opinions and beliefs based on perceptions, experiences and information we have at the time. It does not mean we have absolute truth. Only truth that is irrefutable is absolute—truths in science and mathematics, for example—based on theories and hypotheses proven beyond a doubt. My understanding of truth is on two planes. First, honesty—speaking truth and being truthful in our relationships and interactions with others helps create respect for and trust in one another.

Then there is Truth on a deeper level involving the transcendent. "Significant if unverifiable truths" are revealed in spiritual and psychological principles and in philosophy; myths; music; literature and art, as well as in nature and the universe, inspiring, motivating, enriching and sustaining us beyond measure. Often, Beauty and Goodness can be discovered in these expressions—all there for us to decipher what we see, read, hear, and reflect upon, understand and share—the meaning and mystery within them.

Beauty * Goodness * Truth

My three favorite things are often indistinguishable from one another as are the threads woven into a rich and brilliant tapestry, with power to pass into our purer mind—not only lightening the burden of this unintelligible world, but also rendering it more intelligible. We can be grateful for these three blessings.

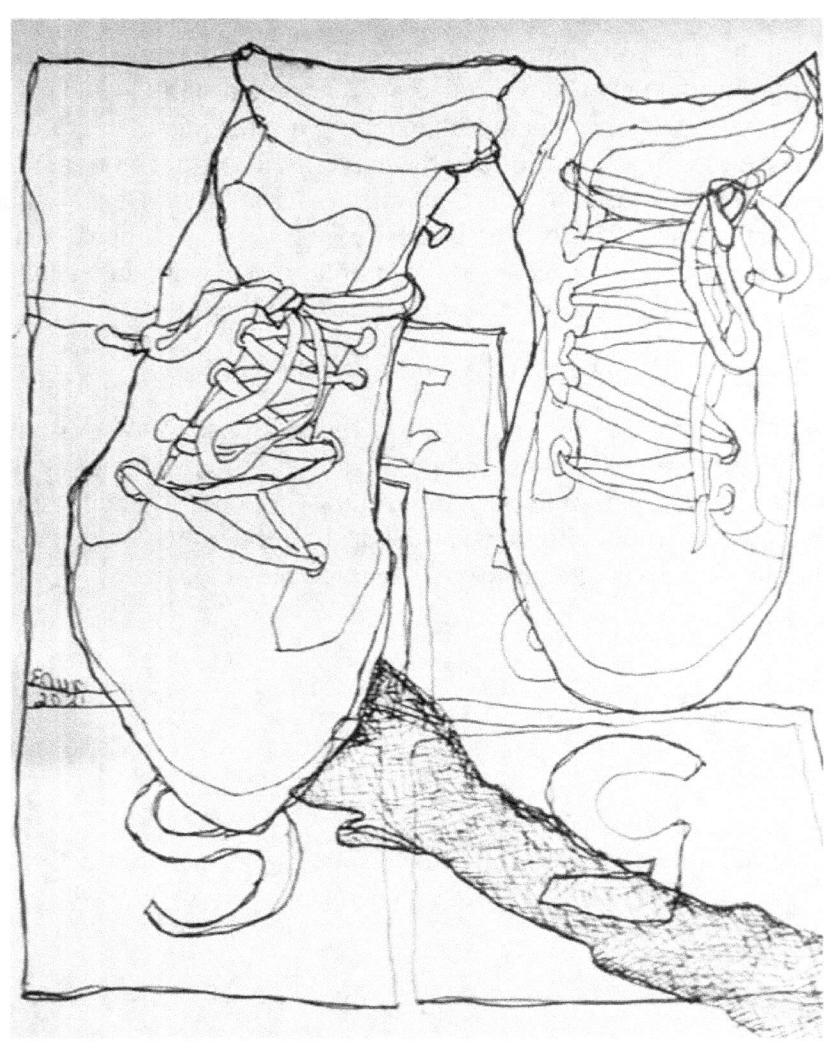

"Leg Drawings" ink   *Anne Chase*

AFTER

~ *John Yamrus*

the rain,

reading Kerouac,

listening
to Cole Porter
playing quiet in the room,
there's
even birds
singing outside the window,

the
only thing
missing here

is
you.

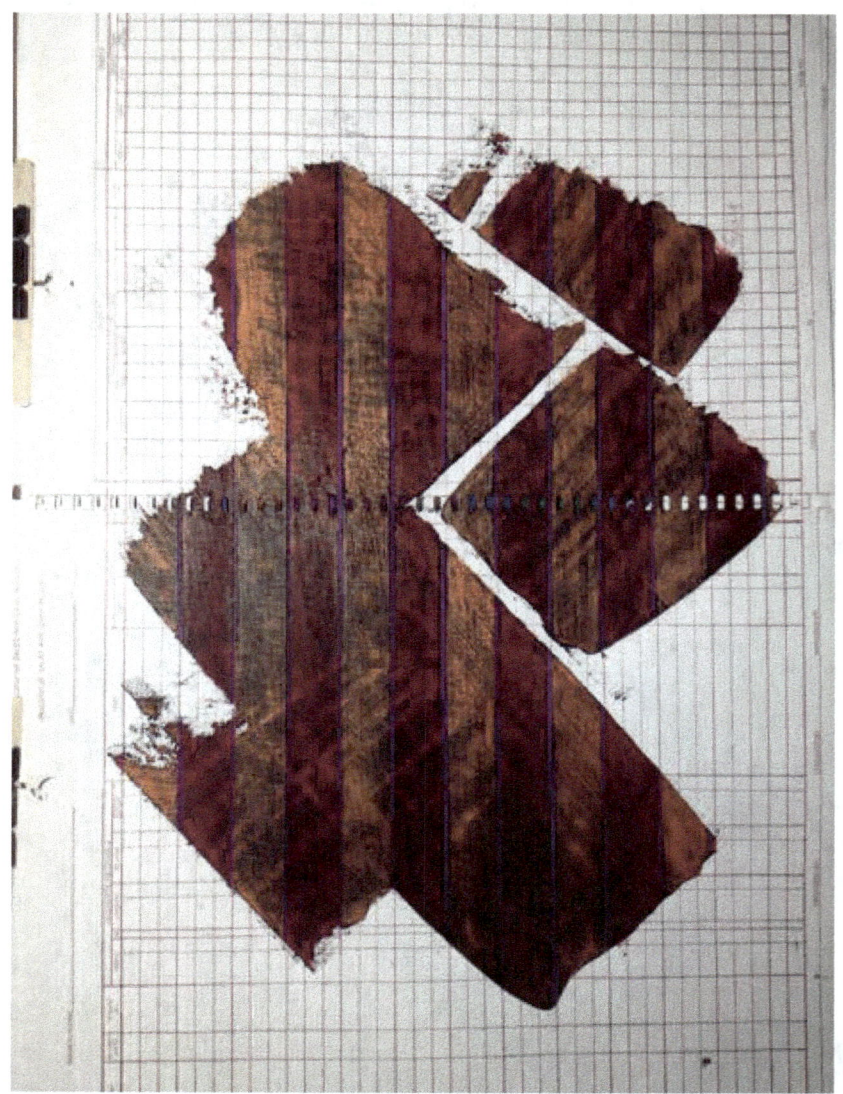

"Untitled" drawing   *Ron Schira*

I SAT IN THE SUN ROOM

~ *John Yamrus*

reading
old books…
juvenile books, mostly.
stuff from back when i was a kid.

the
latest was
National Velvet,

the one
that got made into
a movie with Mickey Rooney
and a very young Elizabeth Taylor

back in 1944
when i was in grade school.

it wasn't 1944.

it was
probably
the late 50's

and my mother
used to let me
stay home sick all the time from school.

there was
even a year

when i came
this close to getting held back

because
i racked up
so many sick days,

but
they couldn't
keep me back because
i was quiet and had good grades,

and

anyway,
like i said
i used to stay
home from school

while
my father
drove a delivery truck,

and
my mother
worked in one of
the many dress factories
that crowded the neighborhood.

my
grandparents
lived right across the street,

and
my grandmother
used to come and check on me at lunch,

bringing
jars of canned cherries

from
the tree they had,

and
i would sleep on the couch

watching movies on tv,

and
i remember
National Velvet being one.

but
i didn't like it very much
because there wasn't any

shooting in it,

and
it was
just for kids.

but

it was
the only thing on,

so, i watched it.

the book
(and the movie)
is about a girl who's skinny and frail

and
a horse
that's big and tough

and
the girl wants
to run it in a race,
only the race isn't open to girls.

reading it now,
it's a pretty good book

and it
takes me back
to those days in 1959
when i got to stay home from school

and
lay on the couch
eating a great big bowl of cherries.

and
i had a pillow

and
a blanket

and
the room

and
the world
around me was

warm

and safe

and
good.

ARTISTS' AND AUTHORS' BIOGRAPHIES

Claudia Bahorik, *M.S., P.T., D.O., is currently reinventing herself as a Professional Writing Student at Penn State Berks Campus. Having retired last spring as a family physician, Dr. Bahorik has been involved in writing in one form or another for most of her professional career. She is a writer for The Merchandiser, a weekly local newspaper, and was previously published in Country Magazine, as a ghost writer for a short story told by her mother. She is currently working on a paranormal romance titled "The Seventh Ghost" - a story based on unusual happenings on her Berks County farm.*

Dr. J. Wesley (Wes) Bahorik *joined the faculty of Kutztown University in 1969 where he was employed as a professor of biology and science education until retiring in 1997. Along with his formal profession, Wes has developed experience as a writer and self-taught artist. Items from his more than 200 works in acrylic, oil, charcoal, pastel, watercolor, and pencil have been shown in Pennsylvania, Maine, New Mexico, Virginia, New Hampshire and North Carolina. His focus has been primarily on a realism style with a few forays into abstract and impressionism. Much of his art stems from his career as a biologist and lover of the outdoors, producing works on wildlife, landscape, and hidden imagery.*

Michael Barnett: *For 33 years, Blue Turtle has served the metaphysical and creative community as an intuitive counselor, teacher, and metaphysician. He studied the tarot intuitively directly with Spirit for nine years. Blue Turtle comes from an intuitive Croatian-Serbian-Ukrainian maternal lineage with his paternal line as Ashkenazi-Levite, who cared for the female aspect of God in the wilderness Tabernacle and the Temple in Jerusalem and Norman-Celtic with Native American spiritual influences. His spiritual writings and poetry are published in* <u>Sedona Journal of Emergence</u> *and the* <u>Universalist Herald</u>*. Blue Turtle facilitates intuitive workshops and classes and his Mystery School of Emerging Eternity. He has made his vibrational healing art cards and paintings since 1988.*

Marilyn Basehoar *Beginning at age fourteen, Marilyn Basehoar is both a self-taught and classically trained artist. She has experimented with mixed media, collage, and assemblages in recent years by expanding her use of different, sometimes surprising, materials such as fabric, stones, glass, and other elements. Although those artworks are chaotic and energetic, she is often called back to her love of oil painting floral and still life.*

Virginia Beards *draws from an archive of urban (New York, Philadelphia), suburban (Seattle), rural (Lancaster county, PA), and international experience (Denmark, France, North Africa) plus a considerable literary backlog acquired as a member of the Penn State English Department for twenty-three years. She has published criticism in The Journal of Modern Literature, Twentieth Century Views of Women Writers, and in Critique: Studies in Modern Fiction. Her poetry has appeared in Writing on the Edge (Univ. of California, Davis and in Provoke, #3, the journal of Backlash Press); her short stories in Chester County Fiction. She holds a M.A. from the University of Pennsylvania and a Ph.D. from Bryn Mawr College.*

Jill Beech. *Jill Beech, DVM, is a retired faculty member of the New Bolton large animal facility of the University of Pennsylvania and a recipient of numerous awards and honors for her career in equine research medicine.*

Craig H. Bennett, *author of* <u>Nights on the Mountain</u>, *-a spiritual journey; and* <u>The Stranger in the Mirror</u>.

Krysta Bernhardt *graduated with honors with a B.F.A. in Musical Theater from the University of the Arts. She is an independent artist and has taught piano, voice and dance in the Philadelphia area for over 20 years. She has collaborated on and helped design and publish creative music books for kids as well as self-publishing her own children's activity books.*

Susan Biebuyck: *Nourishing her own creative spirit, Susan Biebuyck majored in studio fine art at Kutztown University in Pennsylvania. She is known for her acrylic, oil, pastel and watercolor painting diversity; she calls herself "an art supplies junky" and works in a variety of media with fluency. Her work demonstrates superb observation and lyrical spirit and has won honors and awards. She is one of the select studio artists at GoggleWorks Center for the Arts in Reading, Pennsylvania. She is the founder & Gallery Director at Studio B, a fine art gallery in Boyertown, PA.*

Maryanne Buschini *earned an Masters of Art from the University of the Arts, Philadelphia PA, and a BFA from Kansas State University. She has studied extensively at Pennsylvania Academy of Fine Arts (PAFA), the Barnes Foundation, Philadelphia, PA and workshops in the US and Ireland. She has been awarded a painting residency at Bethany Arts Community, Ossining, NY. Researching black and white photos, Maryanne interprets images to create narratives of celebration, hard work, family and love.*

Anne Chase *moved from Louisiana six years ago to receive her master's degree from the Pennsylvania Academy of Fine Arts. She fell in love with both Reading and GoggleWorks Center for the Arts; she decided to stay. She works in several mediums and tries to evoke emotion in her work.*

Albert Ciervo *fell in love with the texture and mobility of plaster with a hands-on understanding of fresco painting. On this old-world ground he perfects a new-world modern style of painting. He is a much-loved fixture of ol' country Berks County who has picked up his family and moved to metropolitan Philadelphia. He declares, "I have 2 daughters who think I'm cool, a wife who loves my cooking, I get to live in this great place with people I love. I cook, paint, drink and travel!"*

Cathryn Clinton *is the author of the critically acclaimed and award-winning* <u>A Stone in My Hand</u>, *as well as* <u>The Calling</u>, *her first novel, which was named a "Publisher's Weekly Flying Start." She graduated with an MFA in Creative Writing from Vermont College and lives in southeastern Pennsylvania. Cathryn believes, "If we can still ourselves to listen to our hearts and our communities, we will find the way to love."*

Tony Cocuzza *has been a "Poet" only 10 years. He has been more prolific as a music reviewer for 33 years in newspapers and a current blog. He has been a featured poet sponsored by Berks Bards at the Goggleworks and also at the Shillington Library where "Nobody "Shooshed" Me!"*

Amanda Lee Condict *is an illustrator and designer, first working as a fashion illustrator for a department store, then an art director of a monthly magazine and finally operated a design and illustration studio. She lectures in the fashion department at Albright College; teaches art at Yocum Institute; operates Vincent van BYO, a painting party studio; and paints murals.*

Rachel Conrad *Always looking for ways to quiet the scream of inspiration, the Holy Spirit nudged her toward photography. She uses her imagination and unusual fears as an asset to her imagery. Through her images, stories unfold inviting the viewer to join her on a journey of examination, dreams, and self-exploration. Her biggest hope is for the viewer to use his/her imagination and grow along with her.*

Carole Croll *is a former elementary ELL (English Language Learner) teacher. She grew up in Schwenksville and has recently returned to the area after spending the previous twenty-four years living in Chicagoland. The Midwest was a difficult transition for someone who loves hills and trees, but in response to many long and solitary walks, she discovered the wonder of the prairie and the bliss of creating poetry about it. Her devotion to the art and craft of writing continues, and she remains inspired by the magnificence of the Pennsylvania landscape and the beautiful complexity of the human heart.*

Kimberlee Dawn *is a working spiritual artist for over 35 years. She has a Masters of Art education, taught art in Daniel Boone School District for 12 years. She has created large local history and world cultures murals with her students. She's been a reiki master, originator and producer of Angel Day Spiritual Holistic Fair for ten years. She lives and maintains a studio in West Reading.*

Stacey Dexter *is a nonfiction writer, musician, singer/songwriter, and animal lover. Her first book,* <u>Eddie: One Dog's Journey from Hobo to a Home</u>*, will be published in 2021.*

Ivy Egger *has had an interest in arts and crafts for as long as she can remember. Her inspirations are sunsets, flowers—the beauties that Nature provides. Her medium of choice is gouache or watercolor.*

Jonathan Egger: *Originally from Pittsburgh, Jonathan now resides near Coatesville, PA, with his wife Ivy, also an artist, and his four-year-old son. Jonathan recently took up short story writing as a hobby during the pandemic and is also dabbling with poetry. A novel about how his family is started is also in the works.*

Steve Fabian *is a Kutztown University BFA graduate Magna Cum Laude. Steve has had the privilege of studying under many wonderful artists. He offers, "I believe that art is all about imagination & feelings. As an artist it is my desire to stir emotions and start discussions. My work is inspired by the natural world, and by human nature."*

Suzanne Fellows *(who lives and breathes creativity) is a painter, printmaker, musician, teacher, designer and gardener. Her work often evokes her feelings about nature, activism, and life She single-handedly saved 20 elephants from extinction with her art project "99 Elephants a Day." She holds a BFA from Kutztown University and an MFA from Vermont College of Fine Art. Suzanne is an acting professor of fine art & design at Reading Area Community College. She is one of the select studio artists at GoggleWorks Center for the Arts.*

Marilyn Fox *recently embraced a new dialog in painting perhaps as a result of cultural climate or a desired a new challenge. Her new work begins with gestural brushwork. She likes to obscure strokes with paint, add more, and scratch away. She explains, "The technique itself can be a bit aggressive; its more assertive than anything I've done before. Through this work, I've developed a new vocabulary; it speaks to me." For the past twenty years, Marilyn was the gallery director/arts administrator at Penn State Berks, in Reading, PA. "Looking back, I have been involved in the arts for four decades."*

Wendy M.C. Fox *is an award-winning amateur photographer living in Elverson, PA. Her photographs have been exhibited in Philadelphia and surrounding areas. She generously donates her work to many local and International non-profit organizations. Her photographs have been part of a blue-ribbon exhibit at the Philadelphia Flower Show and she has also won a Botanical Arts award from the National Garden Clubs, Inc. She has a passion for flowers and holds a Certificate in Floral Design from Longwood Gardens. Wendy is a member of Berks Art Alliance, and the Garden Clubs of Elverson and Uwchlan.*

Andrew Fritz *lives in Fleetwood with his wife and his soon-to-graduate college (and thus also likely to move out soon) daughters. He loves science, history, and occasionally tries his hand at writing fiction. He has two novels in development, one with a co-author and one a solo effort.*

Jen Gittings-Dalton: *After a career of advising and career counseling college students in area colleges, she retired and is enjoying biking around Berks County's back roads! She writes poetry, nonfiction, spends time with friends and family, and likes to explore the beautiful land. Her chapbook, "Pleiades Memoir" was published by FootHills Publishing in 2007. She lives Exeter with her husband Stan and a new cat, Nimbus, and they visit their son and daughter in DC and San Francisco whenever they possibly can.*

Beth Glick *says, "When I was 4 years old I couldn't sit still in church. My mom handed me the church bulletin and a pen to draw on, and I've been doodling ever since. I love the patterns found on old wallpaper and feed sack fabric."*

Heather E. Goodman's *writing has been published in The Sun, The Christian Science Monitor, Fiction, Shenandoah, Gray's Sporting Journal, and the Chicago Tribune, where her story won the Nelson Algren Award. She teaches high school students and lives along the Manatawny with her partner Paul and pups.*

Bob Hakun *earned a BFA in painting at Kutztown University. Bob's always been fascinated by old, weathered, discarded items: some are natural like bones or wood, some man-made like wheels or rusty wire and old things that show the graphic effects of aging. Bob assembles items together in a rough, crude way. The juxtaposition of normally unrelated items creates a new and different story or sculpture that is greater than the sum of the individual parts.*

Walt Hug: *Walt graduated from Antonelli School of Photography in 1976. His began his career as a Medical Photographer for Hahnemann Hospital and Medical School, followed by three years as a photographer for Concepts 80 in Newtown Square, PA. In 1981, he joined Wyeth Pharmaceuticals, as Senior Photographer. He was promoted in 2000, to Manager of Photographic Services, Multimedia Services. Walt's duties at Wyeth included the photography of events, meetings, products, facilities, PR and portraits. He also ran the traditional darkroom and color processing lab prior to the introduction of digital, which he helped convert to digital technology. In 2006, Walt retired from Wyeth but continued shooting for various corporate clients. He now volunteers his time & photography for non-profits. For the past 12 years he has produced and displayed his photographs, including older and current images, with a focus on land & seascapes, abstracts, nature, portraits and architecture, and has shown his work at various galleries & exhibits.*

Angela Izzo *They say laughter is the best medicine, but for Angela it's more than that. Laughter is her lifesaver. Battling major depressive and anxiety disorders her whole life, she found that reframing the difficult situations through humor has helped her navigate through some very hard times. It is her hope, that by using humor in her work, her viewer is able relate to the humorous stories she is trying to tell, regardless of their level of art appreciation.*

James, L.T. *(aka Linda Thomas, aka Linda Thompson), Volunteer Coordinator, Pagoda Writers.*

Nikki Johnson *is the type of free spirit who has become increasingly difficult to pin down as a linear-narrative character. Born in the small Philadelphia suburb of Eagleville, she progressively migrated to larger and larger ponds – first Penn State, then Washington DC, and subsequently Manhattan – to pursue a degree in journalism and build a career as an Internet marketer. Having worked her way up the ladder of a travel-focused digital agency, launched three businesses of her own, and circled the globe.*

Kathryn Keegan *is a member of Schuylkill Writers. She has been writing verse since the age of 16. Presently she is exploring 'hiphop.'*

Kathy Kirk *is a retired teacher of biology & human physiology whose interests span from nature, to health and the human body, to music, crafts and sewing, to skiing and hiking. She is a person who firmly believes that God and science can coexist. She also loves spending time watching her granddaughter grow and develop.*

Marilyn L.T. Klimcho is the Treasurer of Berks Bards, Inc., a grassroots poetry group centered in Reading. In addition to writing poetry, she also writes short stories and has recently tackled writing a screenplay. Her work in short story was nominated for a Pushcart Prize by the Schuylkill Valley Journal.

Jerry Kott is an Artist/Designer/Maker & professional artist from New York City, now residing in the foothills of Lehigh Valley. His career has spanned decades and explored various art markets such as fine art jewelry, sculpture with glass, fabric, leather, wood, concrete and paper as media that he takes to the edge. He's been celebrated in the New York Times and New York Times Magazine, Vogue, ID, Dwell and many international blogs. He and his work are mentioned in the novel American Psycho, which placed him in a category of Modern Americana. He's exhibited in Tokyo, Paris and nationally. He is a recipient of the coveted Accent on Design Award. Jerry sees himself as a modern wildlife artist who explores modernizing the simplicity of the environment to create a second look at beauty we take for granted.

Victoria Lawrence is a visionary painter from Reading, PA, who combines her passion for mountain biking with her art. On any given day, you might find her painting en plein air with her bike in tow, ready to hit the trails while the paint dries. Victoria is represented by Art Plus Gallery, West Reading, PA and The Dreaming Human, Lancaster, PA. She has won several awards for her art and has sold paintings to collectors across the country.

Barrie Maguire is a 1950 Notre Dame graduate, Barrie has been an advertising Art Director, a Creative Director at Hallmark Cards, a writer, editorial illustrator and a painter of Ireland. In 1997 he founded NewsArt.com, the first online source of op-ed illustrations for newspapers all across North America and the world.

Virginia McNamara is retired from a career in mathematics, computer software development, and technical writing. Currently she creates poems and essays inspired by travel experiences, miracles of Nature, and the talented artists and kind souls who continue to shine their light in the world.

Deborah Maguire Meehan graduated from the Art Academy of Cincinnati as a fine arts major, but not too long after graduating, she was hired as a Junior Art Director at an Advertising Agency in Philadelphia. That job determined her path for the next 40 years. Since retiring from advertising in 2014, she's had time to get back to making art. The reason she is doing collages now, with torn newspapers as the main source of color and pattern comes from her love of typography acquired while working in commercial art. Birds are so varied in size and shape and color and geometry that they introduce life and personality into the abstract compositions she creates.

Jim Meehan was born in Brooklyn, N.Y. in 1952. His father was an artist on New York newspapers. Jim graduated from Fordham University with a BS in Psychology and then attended the School of Visual Arts for two years. After art school he worked at the New York Daily News and in advertising. Jim has been printed in many publications and has participated in numerous group shows.

Lesley Misko: *Lesley Huss Misko is a retired Boyertown Area Senior High School (BASH) English teacher and department chair. A native of New York City, she holds a BA in English from Queens College, City University of New York, and an MS in English Education from Syracuse University. During her 35 years of teaching 11th and 12th grade English, she was active at the state and national levels in scholastic journalism and advised the award winning BASH student newspaper,* Cub, *in addition to chairing the school's program for intellectually gifted students. An occasional writer for Patch.com, she resides with her husband, Robert, has a son, Sean, and two cats, Barry and Fiona.*

Lisa Mitchell *has found joy through writing ever since childhood. Much of her inspiration is found in nature, reveling in its strength and beauty. As an amateur photographer, she also enjoys photographing nature's beauty. Professionally, Lisa has been working in the newspaper industry since high school. For the past 15 years, since 2006, Lisa has worked for MediaNews Group in various roles including reporter, editor and managing editor, covering community news, features and events in the Berks County area.*

Joann Moy's *work expresses the innate tendency to seek connections with nature and other forms of life, a hypothesis known as biophilia, introduced by Edward O. Wilson. Seeking to find this connection, this commonality among humanity--then and now--she paints her abstract figures in all colors and poses. Not content with one "signature \ style," she offers landscapes that capture the radiance of sunsets in bright colors and the light and shadows that fall on fields and meadows.*

Kathryn E. Noska *explains, "My tiny 'worlds of possibility', painted with intimate detail and blended depth, enrich imagination making any view feel accessible, real, and huge. I paint subjects symbolizing positive qualities of human nature to understand 'why,' offer visual delight, and connect us with our story."*

Clemson Page, *practicing attorney living in Wyomissing, PA, graduate of Dartmouth College and Villanova University Law School, began his law practice in Reading in 1977. His novel,* Up Home, *1903-1909, was published in 2007 and is listed on Amazon.com. He is a devotee of the Scottish Highland Bagpipe and Celtic culture in general.*

Jillian Wright Prout *obtained a BFA from Kutztown University, studied under Myron Barnstone in Old Masters techniques. She loves to paint in watercolor, oils, and egg tempera. Jillian has been a proud member of Studio B since its inception.*

Phil Repko *is a career educator in the PA public school system who has been writing for fun and no profit since he was a teenager. Phil lives with his wife Julie in Gilbertsville and is the father of three outstanding children, two of whom are also poets and writers. He vacillates between poetry and prose, as the spirit beckons, and is currently working sporadically on a novella and a memoir.*

Theresa Rodriguez *is the author of three books of poetry, including* Sonnets, *a collection of sixty-five sonnets (Shanti Arts, 2020).*

Christine Ross: *Bookworm, check! Nature geek, check! From sun-baked city streets to night skies and all the people-watching in between - absorbed into a curious psyche, Christine taps her words from whatever liquid pours through the pen.*

Ashley Rupert, *a student and ROTC cadet at Boyertown Area Senior High School, began writing poetry when she was 10 years old after the unexpected passing of my best friend and has used her poetry as an outlet ever since in hopes of bringing some much-needed light into the world so frequently perceived from the shadows of our troubles.*

Michael Schiffman *is a 78-year-old poet still trying to get better. His work has appeared in anthologies and journals including* Rise!, *an anthology about work and labor,* The Poetry of Yoga, volume two, *and also* These Fragile Lilacs, Stepaway Magazine, Off-Course Journal," *and* The Write Launch. *He resides proudly in downtown Reading.*

Ron Schira: *Over the course of two and a half decades, artist and art critic Ron has written for the* Reading Eagle *newspaper, publishing a significant 1502 articles in the Greater Berks and Lehigh Counties, along with a few selected shows in Philadelphia and New York City. Writing for them and a handful of other publications, he has covered art events in every museum, art center, commercial gallery, school, college, studio, atelier, street fair, restaurant and garage to give recognition to the visual art community as well as voice to the arts. In 2005, he was invited by Columbia University to be included in a published list of the most read arts writers in the United States. Prior to his work as a critic, aside from the numerous exhibitions of his paintings and various curatorial projects, he has been on the recruitment board of the East Penn Emerging Artists Program and the Pagoda Gallery Installation Committee for the Berks Arts Council. Since the mid nineteen seventies, he has been an integral cultural proponent of the area, actively participating and advocating for the arts. He recently received a Life Achievement Award from the Yocum Institute for Arts Education.*

Sandra Seaman: *Creating helps to ground her and find meaning when the world may appear to be meaningless. She has explored many kinds of creativity in her life. She had a brief love affair with hand weaving. Then a long fifteen-year relationship with lampwork glass bead making and jewelry making. Then on to writing and painting. she has always felt that the circle of creating is not truly complete if she don't share her work with others.*

Jane E. Stahl *currently serves as Director of Community Relations for Studio B following 35 years of sharing a love of literature, writing, and speaking with junior high and high school students and a love of teaching with fellow teachers and the community. Following their dream of living in an artistic community, Jane and her husband Paul founded Boyertown's Bear Fever community art project that ultimately led her into collaboration with fine artist Susan Biebuyck and the establishment of Studio B. So many projects, so little time! Jane hopes someday to take the time to selfpublish a collection of her thoughts and experiences.*

JD Stahl *loathes labels, but in this "go-round" of his many lives he's a teacher, a life coach, a musician, and lover of language. Challenging accepted norms, led by logic and love and an eternal quest for truth, J.D. infuses good intentions toward the recovery and self-discovery of those whose life paths cross his own. For his own evolution, J.D. is constantly seeking ascension towards universal concepts and answers encompassing this world and the next. His own mentor is his beloved canine Ginger. JD has published companion books of his own poetry:* Fragments of Time: The Dark *and* Fragments of Time: The Light. *You can find his 60-episode "Safe in This Moment" podcast on YouTube in which he confronts the conundrums of life and offers inspiration in encouraging enlightenment through critical thinking.*

Hilary Swingle *(1983) Salt Lake City, Utah: this is where she currently works and resides. She is a figurative realist oil painter. Her most recent portraits are autobiographical and explore the threads of her social anxiety using symbolism and highly detailed compositions. She is represented by 33 Contemporary Gallery, Chicago.*

Taku, *known as* **VaChikepe**, *a poet from Zimbabwe with 15 years writing experience, finds beauty in all understandings and wishes "joy" to readers. Latest Book:* Mental Gymnastics *available on www.amazon.com*

Theodore Thomas, *retired engineering executive and Korean War veteran, traveled the world sketching, writing, and photographing his experiences over a working lifetime, drawing inspiration to create a body of pastel paintings that preserve his memories. Some have historical importance. Ted Thomas, Volunteer Coordinator, Pagoda Writers*

Nelvin Vos *is an emeritus professor of English at Muhlenberg College and lives in the village of Maxatawny.*

Merrill Weber: *Merrill Weber's paintings represent the place where her love of life's small pleasures and her passion for painting intersect. She is determined to bring more beauty and happiness into the daily lives of others through her art. Drawing inspiration from everyday living, her engaging work has been described as imaginative, playful and filled with energy and hope. Merrill's goal in painting is to create a conversation with the viewer via her canvas, allowing her to preserve and share in the joy of the moment.*

Lauralynn White *imposes her vision of humanity on the natural world. Integrating human forms in landscape, she illuminates dark places and celebrates the sacredness of all things. Her belief in the necessity of living in harmony with nature is expressed through this sublime and powerful fusion. Lauralynn graduated from Savannah College of Art and Design, Savannah, GA (BFA 1990 illustration/art history). She is Curator/Director of the Contemporary Art Gallery, Chautauqua, NY, instructor at Chautauqua Special Studies, and former Gallery Director at GoggleWorks Center for the Arts, Reading, PA (2010-2018). She has exhibited widely and holds memberships in NAWA and VACI. She currently lives and works in Chicago, IL.*

Aressa V. Williams *is the youngest of fourteen siblings, a Howard University gradu-*

ate, and a retired English professor. She enjoys napping, interpreting dreams, reading poetry, and sky-watching. The poetess believes writing is free therapy.

Sandra Williams is author of <u>Moss on Stone: a historical novella</u> and <u>Time and Tide: a collection of tales</u>. She has published articles in <u>New View</u> magazine (UK), and has written PR pieces, brochures and newsletters for non-profits. She was co-chair for the first writers' conference on Cape Ann, MA, The Dogtown Writers Festival: Finding Words in Place and has facilitated poetry workshops in association with Gloucester Writers Center in MA.

Daniella Yacono is known for her abstracted and figurative oil paintings as well as evocative charcoal works on paper. The work translates the nature of relationships and the mystery and fragility of the natural world into rich imagery. History, memory, and myth blend into one pictorial narrative in her paintings.

John Yamrus: In a career spanning 50 years as a working writer, John Yamrus has published 30 books...25 volumes of poetry, 2 novels, 2 volumes of non-fiction and a children's book. He has also had more than 2,000 poems published in magazines and anthologies around the world. Selections of his work have been translated into several languages, including Spanish, Swedish, French, Japanese, Italian, Romanian, Albanian, Estonian and Bengali. His poetry is taught in numerous colleges and universities.

The End

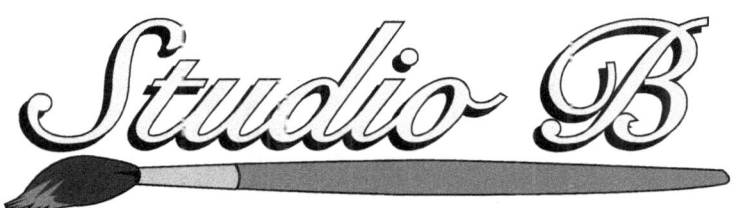

"The Little Gallery That Does."

www.ingramcontent.com/pod-product-compliance
Lightning Source LLC
Chambersburg PA
CBHW071536220526
45469CB00003B/803